How to Grow a Novel

By the Same Author

Novels

The Husband
The Magician
Living Room
The Childkeeper
Other People
The Resort
The Touch of Treason
A Deniable Man
The Best Revenge

Nonfiction

A Feast for Lawyers
Stein on Writing

Plays

Napoleon (also called *The Illegitimist*)
(New York and California
Dramatists Alliance Prize, "best full-length play of 1953")

A Shadow of My Enemy
(National Theater, Washington, D.C., and Broadway, 1957)

How to Grow a Novel

THE MOST COMMON MISTAKES WRITERS MAKE AND HOW TO OVERCOME THEM

SOL STEIN

St. Martin's Press New York

 For information address St. Martin's Press, 175 Fifth Avenue, New York, N.Y. 10010.

Library of Congress Cataloging-in-Publication Data

Stein, Sol.
How to grow a novel : the most common mistakes writers make and how to overcome them / Sol Stein.
p. cm.
ISBN 0-312-20949-5
1. Fiction—Authorship. 2. Fiction—Technique. 3. Creative writing. I. Title.
PN3365.S82 1999
808.3—dc21
99-36922
CIP

First Edition: December 1999

10 9 8 7 6 5 4 3 2 1

For Edith

CONTENTS

ACKNOWLEDGMENTS

It takes courage to edit an editor and publish a publisher. I want to thank Marian Lizzi for undertaking both tasks with courage and skill. Patricia Day corrected my memory of some past events, for which I am grateful. I was once again fortunate in being able to tap Elizabeth Stein's judgment in the course of writing. I remain indebted beyond easy measure to the writers, famous, infamous, and not yet known, as well as the teachers, readers, and students with whom I shared a life of editorial work and joy, and from whom I learned much of what is in the book.

Women usually outnumber men among my students, readers, and friends. I trust they will forgive me for using a male pronoun to stand for both genders. Saying "he or she" repeatedly is a distraction for both writer and reader.

PREFACE: FOR THE READER WHO IS ALSO A WRITER

Come sit. We need to talk. I have been working with writers for more than forty years, side by side, one on one, always with the intent of getting a book into shape for successful publication. Most of these authors had publishing contracts and deadlines. Some of them were famous or became so as a result of their work. A fair number wrote books that will surely survive into the new millennium.

In 1990, after more than a quarter of a century as editor-in-chief of a book-publishing firm, I also began to work with eager newcomers, writers who had not yet published fiction. I conducted workshops at the University of California and elsewhere, speaking at writers' conferences, talking to groups. In my Chapter One workshops, mainly for writers who had attended my university lecture course, about two dozen writers would gather each week around a large conference table to learn by editing. Most of the newcomers were successful professionals in other fields (law, medicine, teaching, business) who in midlife turned to writing fiction and were surprised at how complex the craft is, and were pleased to learn how many solutions had already been devised by other writers. Some of the participants were successful nonfiction writers who were new only to fiction writing. What a reward when one, the author of thirty-four nonfiction books, writing fiction for the first time, won the short-story competition at the Santa Barbara Writers Conference.

We called these workshops Chapter One because all of the participants worked intensively in perfecting each writer's first chapter in turn. By the end of three months, each participant had worked under my supervision on twenty-four first chapters. In this way they learned the craft of fiction to the point where they could then go on and revise the rest of their chapters on their own.

In many workshops writers read their material out loud, which has disadvantages. Some writers read well, others poorly. Good writing badly read is boring. Faulty writing read with flair can sound a lot better than it is. In the Chapter One workshops, we didn't read aloud for another reason also. *Readers see a writer's work as words on a page, and that is how writing should be judged.* Therefore every week in our seminar, three writers would each bring in two dozen copies of their first chapters. After the instruction that preceded every work session, each of us around the table would read *and edit* the same first chapter. These writers were learning to revise by editing the work of their peers, putting to use instruction they had just learned or reviewed. We'd discuss a chapter's virtues and faults. I might suggest how a fault could be remedied or a virtue enhanced. Line-editing suggestions, page by page, were made by members of the group. I am totally deaf in my left ear, and if an editing suggestion by a participant seemed wrong, I would tap my deaf ear, and then offer a correction. I was not a traffic cop, but in my familiar role as editor-in-chief approved or amended the work of less experienced editors. At the end of a semester, each writer's first chapter had been revised to as near perfection as the writer's talent and experience would permit. Best of all, the participants now had knowledge and editing experience to bring to the rest of their own manuscripts, and to whatever they would write in the future.

Normally, writing courses are designated as being for beginners or for advanced work. Writers are segregated by their talent and experience. I prefer to mix successful writers with talented newcomers. The newcomers' hunger for craft and experience helps energize the more successful, reminding them of craft they'd forgotten or overlooked. A writer's learning experience, like a physician's, never ends.

Frustrated that I could not conduct seminars in many places at once, I cloned myself in several computer programs that enabled writers to plug me into their ears, as it were, as if I were editing their work one-on-one. The results were rewarding, and in some cases spectacular. To reach out to still others, I wrote *Stein on Writing*, which dealt with the essential craft of both fiction and nonfiction. Why then this book?

In *Stein on Writing* I dealt with essential craft techniques, but not in the depth possible in face-to-face meetings. I was urged to write a book in which I could deal with the most important *recurrent* problems in the same depth as I would in an extended meeting with an individual author, using examples from a variety of successful novels, including some from my experience as an editor.

Some of what I intended to do was a gamble, but who gambles more than the writer whose initial obstacle is a blank piece of paper on which he hopes to make invented characters come alive? My most intensive one-on-one experience was with Elia Kazan, director of five Pulitzer Prize–winning plays, including Arthur Miller's best, *Death of a Salesman*, and Tennessee Williams's best, *A Streetcar Named Desire*. These works by the two playwrights, perhaps the best of the American theater in the second half of the twentieth century, are extraordinarily different from each other. What they had in common was Kazan as their director. For his work in film,

Kazan received two Academy Awards—for his direction of *Gentlemen's Agreement* and *On the Waterfront*—and, in 1999, by unanimous vote of the board of the Academy of Motion Picture Arts and Sciences, a rare honorary Oscar for his life's work in film.

I spent nearly every day for five months working on a novel by Kazan that another publisher had rejected as uneditable. That long editorial process was a big risk for both author and editor. Kazan as director was the boss of a play or film, and it required courage to turn the directorial role over to someone else when it came to his writing. That the gamble was worth it was evidenced by *The Arrangement*'s long run on the bestseller lists, where it stayed at number one for thirty-seven consecutive weeks. Later in this book I propose to take the reader to some examples from those five months of work on that ostensibly uneditable novel, which was improved to the point where it became a record-breaking best-seller. I will also offer details of my work with newcomers to fiction who have not yet published, to convey as much as possible of the entire range of editorial comment.

The function of an editor is to help a writer achieve the writer's intentions. In providing examples from other writers' works, I am sometimes guessing as to the writer's intentions. The only writer whose intentions I know firsthand are my own. And so I will also use examples from my work, for which, in reversed roles, I had the benefit of other editors who had the courage to edit an editor. I trust the result will produce some of the benefits of close work that makes one-on-one editorial consultation rewarding.

The first section of the book is titled "The Responsibilities of the Writer." The second section is titled "The Responsibilities of the Publisher." As one of the very few who have spent a lifetime as both writer and publisher of writers, I hope to clarify what each of the parties should consider on the hazardous road to publication.

Before we begin, I should like to offer a definition. A writer is someone who cannot not write. By "writing" I mean creative writing, not messages to a friend. It may be useful to think of fiction writing as preparing a gift for a stranger, the unseen reader we hope to please. The definition "a writer is someone who cannot not write" may seem clumsy, but acquaintance will reveal its eccentric virtue. Consider the opposite: a nonwriter is someone who can write or not, who does not have the drive and need to put words to paper.

A writer is someone who looks forward to the day's work, even if it lasts only an hour or two before the writer has to dash to a job that supports him and his family until such happy time that the writing itself may be economically rewarding. On those days when external circumstances prevent his writing, a writer feels a hollowness, an absence, a longing. A writer is a person who knows that whatever one first sets down is a *draft*, that drafts are palimpsests ready for change the next day and the next day until they can no longer be improved. True, some writers suffer while writing. I regret their pain, and am glad to report that as one masters the craft, the pain ebbs, and the pleasure of being able to control the result can bring the second-greatest pleasure of life, the creation of text that arouses the emotions of distant readers.

I have occasionally worked with writers whose primary lust is for money and fame. Few who have that as their primary impulse succeed, and if they do, it is as carpenters of transient experience rather than as creators of characters who may endure in a way that mortals can't. The joy men and women feel when parenting a newborn who they hope will outlive them is akin to the joy a writer feels when he creates characters who take shape, grow, and in time become able to stand on their own feet and take their place in the world. It all starts each day with the necessity of putting words on paper.

Liars say they write only for themselves. We do not create children solely or mainly for ourselves; they are eventually independent extensions of ourselves released to the world. And so is the writer's writing. It is meant to be published, which means put out to the world with pride. It is for that writer that this book is written.

Now, in our imaginations, let us sit side by side, examining the most common serious faults in other people's fiction in order to benefit yours.

—Sol Stein
Scarborough
April 1999

The Responsibilities of the Writer

ONE

The Reader Is Looking for an Experience

What in the world does writing fiction have to do with courtesy?

Lack of courtesy may be the chief fault that distinguishes unsuccessful writing from the most successful. Courtesy is often confused with etiquette, and shouldn't be. Etiquette is a code of behavior considered correct in a given society, do you or do you not keep your left hand in your lap while using a fork or a spoon with your right? Many of the "rules" of behavior are frivolous and deserve to be ignored. I am talking about courtesy, which is sometimes poorly defined in dictionaries as "polite behavior." Courtesy is one of the more important elements in human conduct. It calls for a consideration of the needs and wants of another person.

Etiquette is a man opening a door for a woman. Courtesy is a woman opening a door for a man carrying packages in both arms. The difference between etiquette and courtesy is enormous. For example, in love making, etiquette—that is, expected behavior under a given code—may be nice or irrelevant. Courtesy toward a lover, understanding and playing to the needs of one's partner, is essential. Courtesy is also essential to writing, and, sadly, much overlooked by writers who do not consciously consider what the reader may be feeling at any particular point in a story or novel. Here and elsewhere in this book I will be describing techniques of pleasing the writer's partner, the reader; for the pleasured reader will be grateful and loyal to the writer, buying each book and looking forward to the next one.

What is it then that the reader wants?

The reader of fiction may welcome insight and information, yes, but is primarily seeking *an experience different from and greater than his or her everyday experiences in life*. When a child claps its hands with joy at the promise of being read a story, the child is anticipating pleasure, an experience that excites its imagination and is unlike the child's daily routines. Children treasure their books. The sight of those books reflects the memory of experiences that were full of wonder. When a child segues through the shock of puberty into the teenage years, the wonder generated by stories doesn't cease. Teenagers are fascinated by tales of extraordinary experiences, adventure, fantasy, science fiction, by the good winning out against the bad only after horrendous obstacles have been overcome. When the teenager passes into adulthood, his expectations from fiction are greater. The new adult is less tolerant of coincidence, cartoonish characters, overly familiar plots, static descriptions, speechifying, boring passages, all of which get in the way of an experience so involving that the reader is not aware of turning pages and cannot leave until there are no more pages left to turn.

Fiction involves the creation of characters and events that originally resided only in the writer's mind. The writer creates a vehicle for transporting his characters to the reader's imagination, and does so with techniques that enable the reader to believe that the fiction is true. In the 1970s my wife and I used to visit a resort in Jamaica called Round Hill for a couple of weeks in the cold depth of New York's winter. Round Hill had a number of attractions besides the weather. It was once a watering hole for publishers, and as a relatively young publisher I could meet an occasional senior competitor under noncompetitive social circumstances. More important, the guests came not only from the States, but from Europe, and we always seemed to meet people who became friends whom we would continue to see on both sides of the Atlantic. I particularly liked a cottage that had a tree house the size of a living room, with tropical vines that visibly grew inches each day. Luckily, the titled Englishwoman who owned the cottage had read a novel of mine called *The Magician*, and this happy coincidence cleared the way for me to rent her cottage. Each two cottages shared a swimming pool. On one such trip, we arrived by air in a sweltering afternoon, and quickly put on swim clothes and headed for the pool.

As I was doing a few laps, I noticed the couple from the neighboring cottage sitting at the far end of the pool. The man was consuming books, by which I mean he was going at first one book and then another so voraciously that he seemed like a hungry man presented with his first food after a period of starvation. I recognized some of the covers. These were substantial books, not a summer's beach reading. A publisher of books who spies a voracious reader immediately has his antennae up. I stopped swimming at my neighbors' end of the pool and, neck deep in water, introduced myself. My neighbors proved to be from Glasgow, he Scottish, his wife English. I later learned that he was the third-generation, reluctant CEO of Goldberg's, Scotland's biggest department store chain, and also Chairman of the Scottish Symphony Orchestra and the author of plays. We chatted a bit and I asked, "Do you ever read fiction?"

"No," he said. "I am only interested in what is true."

I have wasted a good portion of my life trying to reform people, but couldn't resist getting out of the pool, and returning within minutes with a paperback copy of Jerzy Kosinski's masterpiece, *The Painted Bird*, that I happened to have in my briefcase. Without much ado, I passed the book to him, and he politely put aside the book he was reading and started *The Painted Bird.* After a while, he came over with an urgent question: "Is this true?"

I swam over to his side of the pool and said, "Do you think it's true?"

He finished the book before dinnertime. I loaned him another novel, which he took gladly. I had made a convert who read only what is true.

The opposite of true is "made up." How disappointing it is when a writer presents the draft of a story to a friend, and the friend says, "It sounds made up." My objective in this book is to help novelists perfect their skill in making the reader turn pages, to forget that he is reading, to live among characters that once resided only in the writer's head and now seem true and memorable to strangers.

"Memorable" is not an idle word. Our brains register, record, and preserve the moments of books that have generated the most-intense experiences. When I was five or six years old, a doctor ordered me to bed with an illness I don't believe I had. While my mother had taught me to read at four, I was still being read to by her, and, when she was at work, by a sitter. At one point they took turns reading to me a book that contained a villainous Indian who had a third eye in the center of his forehead and could therefore watch his prisoner with that eye even when he slept. Being watched night and day was a terrifying thought long before George Orwell's *1984.* The story of the Indian terrified me so much that I begged my mother to throw the book away. I was relieved when she told me that she had disposed of the offending volume.

Some months later, no longer confined to bed, I was walking

down the hallway where my parents' books were shelved and noticed a familiar binding poking its nose out from behind other books. I plucked it from the shelf. It was the book about the three-eyed Indian! I was instantly overwhelmed by the terror I had felt when it was read to me. My mother had betrayed me. When she saw my reaction, this time she got rid of the book, in part at least to rebuild our bridge of trust.

A book that's been shelved after reading is like an object that is ready to come alive again when we notice it. A book that has provided a moving experience has taken on some magical property, much like a keepsake that reminds you of an out-of-the-ordinary experience long ago. A novel that has done its job will not be discarded because it has been used. That priestly alchemist, the writer, has turned words into memorable experience.

We attribute nonmaterial properties even to books we haven't read. There was a time in the 1960s and 1970s when young people scorned property, things you would take with you if you moved. When it came to books, they preferred paperbacks to hardcovers not just because of price, but because you could leave them behind when you shifted elsewhere. In 1974 my publisher sent me on a twenty-one-city tour to publicize my new novel. In Los Angeles, UCLA assembled students from a number of writing classes in a lecture hall where I was to speak. The instructor finished introducing me by holding up a copy of my new novel. I took it from him gently, and with a practiced movement suddenly tore the hardcover book in half. Some students screamed. Why? The book was not a baby I was tearing limb from limb. It was a physical object made of paper, ink, and glue. No one in the audience had yet had a chance to read it. The response from that audience demonstrated that the students spontaneously felt I was destroying something special.

When a totalitarian state wants to attack the culture of a people, it makes a bonfire of its books, a source of pain even to people who have not read most of the volumes heaped onto the fire. Books are symbolic not only of the pleasures and insights derived from them, but also as the safe harbor of the knowledge that passes from one generation to the next. Burning books is an attempt to stop time, to cut short the progression from monks copying books important to their beliefs, to the end of the twentieth century, when tens of millions of people rely on books as providers of knowledge and extraordinary experience. Why else give twelve hours of life over to a book, which is what we're asking our readers to do?

When the baseball, football, or basketball season is at its height, a considerable portion of the American male population and a not insignificant number of females deploy hours away from work watching their sport on television. What the baseball fan, for instance, hopes for, consciously or not, are the moments of tension and suspense when a ball is hit but not yet caught, when a runner is headed for a base and has not yet reached it. The same applies to other sports as well. The spectator rooting for his hero experiences tension, suspense, anxiety, and pleasure, all the things readers hope for when they turn to a novel. The reader is enjoying the anticipation and excitement that are often worrying in life but a pleasure when they are happening on the ball field or in a book.

What is amazing is the fact that so many writers with a novel in the planning stage give little or no conscious thought to the reader's experience. They need look no further than sports to understand that *the spectator seeks the excitement that does not usually occur in daily life.* The joy of winning, even through surrogates, is real. And the displeasure of losing through surrogates is also real. Spectators cheer their favorites and boo their antagonists, as they do, figuratively, in fiction. And if a favored character is trounced, the reader feels the same sadness felt by a sports enthusiast whose team has just lost. But let us remember that when a team—even the team we are rooting for—is winning too easily, our enjoyment of the game decreases. What the sports spectator and the reader enjoy the most is a contest of two strong teams, a game whose outcome hangs in the balance as long as possible.

The reader is the "customer" of fiction, a notion that can easily be disparaged when it is misconstrued. The need to give pleasure to a reader is not a license to produce hackwork. Kingsley Amis once said that he didn't think he'd ever written anything designed purely as a sop to the reader. "But," he added, "I always bear him in mind, and try to visualize him and watch for any signs of boredom or impatience to flit across the face of this rather shadowy being, the Reader."

True, a large public exists for trash, does that mean writers must or should write transient works? Most writers of so-called popular fiction (the term is wrong; some literary fiction is quite popular) are content to use stock characters, words that are not quite right, cliches, awkward rhythms, phony plot twists, and melodramatic coincidences. A minority of the authors of transient fiction bring some literary values into their popular work, and are rewarded with a wider audience. Every kind of fiction is enhanced by the author's use of precision and nuance in his choice of words. Readers value and remember extraordinary characters long after tricky plots are forgotten. At the same time, it serves us to recognize that certain elements common to transient works are necessary for all fiction, of whatever reach. For instance, the tension and conflict that readers of suspense fiction enjoy have been essentials in theater and fiction since the first storytellers addressed their audiences across a fire.

There's the rub. The original storytellers could see the reactions of their audiences. If these listeners were not held in thrall by what they were hearing, they would doze off right in front of the storyteller, or worse, kill him. Today, the playwright has a sense of his audience's reaction. He knows what holds it silent and spellbound, and also what lapses in the writing or performance cause the coughing and restlessness that signal a drop in attention. But writers of novels and films do not see their audiences. The audience must therefore be imagined. And we bring to that image what we have learned about audiences, they enjoy in fiction what they often deplore in life: anxiety, tension, suspense, and conflict. We ignore those needs of the audience at our peril.

There is an additional benefit to understanding the reader's need for high experience. The more involving that experience is for the reader, the more likely the reader is to tell others, thus beginning the valuable chain reaction called "word of mouth," which is responsible in large measure for the creation of bestsellers as well as the evolution of long-term publication of books that we have come to call "classics."

It is an astonishing fact that many experienced as well as inexperienced writers with whom I have worked have not given much thought to what the reader is experiencing in each scene of a novel. Perhaps it is because courtesy—considering the experience of the reader—is often ignored in dry schooling, where literature is examined for structure and technique more than effect. Consider also that many newcomers to writing want to get something off their chests, which leads them to imagine the audience as passive receptors rather than active enjoyers of a heightened experience fashioned for them by the writer.

How and when can writers deal with the reader's experience? Those writers who attempt to consider the reader's experience *while writing* usually fail. The time to think about the effect of each sequence is *when planning a scene or revising it.* It is obviously more efficient to plan the reader's experience of a scene before writing it. If one has failed to do that, the experience of the reader needs to be considered when examining the first and subsequent drafts.

How does the writer know if the reader will have an experience when reading a given section? If some time has gone by, if the writing has been allowed to cool, when the writer rereads that scene he will experience some level of the emotion that will be felt by the reader coming upon the scene for the first time. If the writer experiences ennui or nothing, he cannot expect the reader to feel more. That sequence—paying attention to the reader's needs after the scene is written—is wasteful compared to giving thought to the reader's needs before the scene is drafted. To that end, let us consider a number of possibilities.

Writers are sometimes encouraged to write a synopsis of a planned novel for a prospective agent or publisher to interest them in reading the manuscript. This précis is usually a summary of the plot with minimal characterization, and does not allow for conveying the texture of the writing in the book to come. A synopsis works better for transient fiction, thrillers and the like, where the plot counts most, though it seldom conveys how well the book will be written.

I've heard writers and writing teachers argue against synopses on the grounds that making an outline of the events in a book can stifle the writer's imagination, that sometimes the unknown is more productive, that a developed character may "tell" the writer what happens next. I agree to the extent that I would find a detailed synopsis of my plot restrictive. What then do I propose?

My interest is in helping the writer fashion the novel efficiently. Therefore, my recommendation is that the novelist make an outline *of scenes only.* This is for the writer's use, and invaluable if used correctly. In the chapter on suspense in *Stein on Writing* I show the usefulness of the scene outline. With a view toward providing more-detailed guidance, here are some questions to review for each scene.

• **Which character in the scene do you have the most affection for? How can you make the reader feel affection or compassion for that character in this scene?** There are, of course, many ways of doing this. Here is a simple example: The woman who is your protagonist hears a scratching at her door. It is the dog she put out of the room because her unfriendly guest was annoyed by the dog's barking. The guest may have some power over the protagonist. It could be anything—an unpaid debt, a secret discovered. Your protagonist is momentarily torn between the potential annoyance to her guest and the scratching and whining of the dog that wants back in. At that moment in time, the reader doesn't like the guest. When the protagonist goes to the door, lets the dog in, and swoops it up into her arms, the reader is glad and warms to your protagonist for what she did. The goal is to involve the reader's emotion, in this case a feeling of warmth for the central character. Caution: Compassion toward an animal has to be handled gingerly lest it come across as sentimental.

Let's look at a slightly more complex situation. On some flimsy excuse, a daughter is trying to dissuade her mother from attending her high-school graduation because her mother doesn't dress well or speak well. The reader will have empathy for the mother. At the graduation other parents stare at the mother, who is wearing an outrageous hat and whose cheeks are conspicuously rouged. After the ceremony, the mother wants to meet some of her daughter's classmates and their parents, but the daughter, embarrassed by how her mother looks and talks, tries to spirit her away. The mother, glancing over her shoulder at the crowd that includes the people she will now never know, trips and breaks off the heel of one shoe. She now has to hobble along, holding on to her daughter's arm, with her broken shoe in her other hand. The reader will feel for the mother, but may also experience the daughter's embarrassment.

It is those feelings of the reader that the writer is trying to influence by the characterization and events he is creating.

• **Is there a character in this scene who threatens the protagonist subtly or openly, psychologically or physically?** For the reader's interest, whenever possible characters should have an adversarial relationship. Every character has his own "script" in every situation. No two distinct characters are likely to have the same scripts, not a mother and her child, not a husband and wife, not an employer and employee, not even two close friends. To the extent that the writer uses their differences, the scene will come across as dramatic. In the first example cited above, it's easy. The guest is already unfriendly. The guest does not like dogs. The protagonist seems to prefer to calm the dog than to please the guest. An adversarial relationship between protagonist and guest is heightened by the protagonist's choice in favor of the dog. In the second example, the adversarial relationship of mother and daughter is based on class differences, which are at the heart of so much fiction. The point to remember is that if the characters in a scene have different scripts, their actions and dialogue will be adversarial. It is that adversity that heightens the reader's experience.

• **Is the point of view of the scene that of the character who is most affected by what happens in the scene?** You may need to override this question if it doesn't suit the point of view necessary to your story. I put the question to remind you that the reader is most affected *when the character whose point of view you are using is the one most affected by what happens in the scene.*

• **Is the scene described in terms of the action that takes place?** If there is no action, there is no scene. Action connotes something happening. That is not necessarily physical movement. An argument on an ascending curve is an action. In the hands of a skilled writer, a disagreement over something important, handled subtly, is an action. Remember that the reader is not moved by the writer or a narrator telling him what one or another character feels. *The reader is moved by seeing what happens to the characters engaged with each other.* If the only action is minor, the scene will be minor. That should lead you to think whether the scene should have a stronger action, or perhaps be merged with a scene that does. The bit about the dog scratching at the door is not a scene. The real action of the scene is what happens between the protagonist and the unwelcome visitor. In the second example, the tension between mother and daughter at the graduation, done with detail, can be a scene.

You may also want to consider whether every substantial portion of a scene is a necessary part of the main action. Does it contribute to the story? Does it help lead into the main action? Does it raise an unresolved issue and thereby heighten suspense? If it does not do any of these, you might be endangering the tension of the chapter by the inclusion of material that is not germane to your story. For example, the reader does not need to see the mother and daughter coming to the graduation, or the entire graduation ceremony, to experience the friction of the daughter-mother relationship, which is the core of this story. The mother wants to be a celebrant, but the celebration is spoiled for both. The frequent fault of new fiction writers is that they unravel the thread of the story instead of keeping it taut like the gut strings of a tennis racket. To help detect such faults, scene descriptions should be brief. Most writers are tempted to spin out scene descriptions, possibly because their urge is to get on with the writing of the novel. *The value of the scene outline is dependent in part on the simplicity with which the action is stated.* The writer's self-discipline should be engaged to keep the description of each scene brief, even terse. "Harriet comes home to find Chuck isn't there, the baby isn't there, half of Chuck's closet is empty of clothes, and the baby's things are gone." That's the scene outline. It would have no effect on the reader's emotions. It is a synoptic telling of the action. In writing the scene itself, the writer's aim is to quicken the reader's pulse by showing the action bit by tense bit as Harriet goes through the house and slowly realizes her husband has fled with the child. The reader feels *Stop looking as if you expect to find them in another room, they're gone!* At the end of the scene, the reader is desperate to know what Harriet will *do.* That is the writer's clue. Leave the reader in suspense. It is courteous because that's what the reader wants. Start the next chapter in another place, or with another character. If you want to stay in that house, a friend or a neighbor could be at the door, someone on familiar terms with the family. Though in life Harriet would be likely to tell the friend what's happened immediately, you don't want to do that in your story, you want to keep the reader's need to know high. Harriet is trying to keep her personal disaster a secret. The friend is determined to help, to find out what's wrong.

• **Is each scene visible throughout so that the reader can see what's happening before his eyes?** This is important because if action is not visible, you are probably sliding into narrative summary of past events or offstage events, which can lower the reader's experience.

• **Does the ending thrust the reader into the next scene? Does the reader long to find out what happens next?** When you review the order of your proposed (or existing) scenes, your focus should be on what will keep the reader reading from scene to scene. Shelly Lowenkopf, a tough and excellent teacher of writers and conductor of the famed Pirate Workshop at the Santa Barbara Writers Conference, reports that he is forever quoting a terse sentence of mine that I don't remember originating: *Never take the reader where the reader wants to go.* Your job as a manipulator of the reader's emotions is to start the next chapter somewhere else or with a different character, leaving the reader hanging. You are not a nice guy, you are a writer. You are consciously manipulating what the reader feels. *Never take the reader where the reader wants to go.* The essence of book-length suspense is to keep the reader curious, especially at the end of each chapter, and to frustrate the reader's expectation by the way you start the next chapter. There are many variations to this technique. One I've used from time to time is to end a chapter with a tense, *unresolved* happening, and then to start the next chapter quietly. Think of it as the calm before the next storm. That calm at the beginning of a chapter (after the first, of course) increases the tension in the reader.

The points to remember:

The ideal arrangement is to have scene after scene with nothing in between. If you build to a scene, don't let the reader's emotions rest. Salt your buildup with ominous detail. At the end of each chapter, be sure you are thrusting the reader forward to the next chapter, then *don't take the reader where the reader wants to go.*

When fashioning a scene outline, you are not engraving stone. You can always modify the outline as you work—and you will. You can change the order of scenes to increase suspense, you can eliminate scenes in which there is no tension, and you can introduce new scenes prompted by the way your story is developing. Your scene outline is meant to be changed much as a jazz musician will toy with a score. If you've got a lot of changing or transposing to do, you might find it convenient to put each scene description on a 3"×5" card, number the scenes, and test new locations by moving the cards about. One of the useful by-products of this is that when you are finished, you will know that you have absolutely the best order you can come up with for your story.

When you prepare an outline of scenes, each delineating at least one action, examine that list to see if any scene seems far weaker than the rest. Often it will be a scene written for the convenience of the writer, usually to get some information across, instead of for the experience of the reader. That's a cue to cut that scene from your plan and look for an action in another scene that will enable you to get that information across, perhaps in adversarial dialogue. You may need to divide the information between two or more places, but I have yet to find a manuscript where necessary information can't be worked into an active scene in a way that won't seem expository.

The scene outline also provides a means of seeing which scenes—on a comparative basis—seem strongest. Sometimes that will suggest that the strongest scene be moved forward to help captivate the reader earlier. Or if that is not suitable, the strong scene may suggest how to strengthen an existing scene earlier in the book.

A scene outline provides the same opportunity for examining what's most wrong in the story and fixing it before spending months of wasteful writing on chapters that were conceived badly and needed to be excised or changed. The scene-by-scene examination of a proposed novel is a major step in the right direction. When this scene outline has been refined and, if necessary, the order changed, ask yourself about each scene, "What is this scene doing to the reader's emotions?" Write your answer next to each scene description. Keep it in mind before you begin to write that scene. Part of becoming a professional writer is awareness of what you are trying to do each step of the way as well as mastering the techniques necessary to achieve your intentions.

At a discussion among playwrights one night in 1998, I jotted down one phrase I heard several times. *You must reward your audience.* As you review your scene list, ask yourself which of those scenes will be so strong, so good, so memorable that your audience will be rewarded. Think of your fiction as a gift for a stranger, the unseen reader you hope to please. The reader is waiting to be exhilarated by what you do, and to fall in love with your characters. How you help the reader fall in love is the subject of another chapter, but in keeping with what I've taught, not the next one. I'm not going to take you where you want to go . . . just yet.

TWO

Is Conflict a Necessity?

Once upon a time the subject was hunting. Maybe it was the only subject.

It was the time of our ancestors, the hunter-gatherers. Before they knew how to make fires, when it grew dark, it was time to sleep. With the discovery of fire, not only were they able to cook their food, they had a bright place to gather after the day's work was done. There, around the fire, one can assume the men who hunted told what happened on the hunt. At one point, let us imagine, someone back home in the cave or wherever said to the returning hunter, "How was it out there?" The hunter said, "Rough," which served to convey the difficulty of tracking and killing animals with the most primitive of weapons. "Rough" could also serve as a one-word excuse if the hunter didn't bag enough. But the hunter's hungry horde back home wasn't satisfied with "Rough," they wanted details. And so the unsuccessful hunter, possibly to save his own life, had to go into specifics—where he hunted, what he saw and heard, how he tracked an animal, perhaps how a sudden storm or a falling tree impeded the chase, how he had to turn back home empty-handed. He was into telling a story.

If the storyteller wasn't convincing, his listeners might kill him. (Rejection slips are a recent development.)

Perhaps, on occasion, an ambitious younger man would volunteer to join the hunt. His foray might prove successful. He could tell what happened in convincing detail. His evidence was the meat he brought back. He would be applauded. He might soon become the number-one storyteller and get rewards like the successful storytellers of today receive.

The successful hunter, being human, possibly enhanced his story by telling what he would have liked to have happen on the hunt. To impress the audience, he may have recounted dangers that didn't quite happen along with those that did. He would spin out how he dealt with danger, and how he overcame the danger at last.

One can presume that because of the dangers, hunters would go out in groups. They would be witnesses to each other's actions. It is possible that the best hunters were not the best storytellers. Like today. So the hunters might let the best storyteller, perhaps the most insightful among them—or the most convincing liar—speak for them. And they would tolerate his exaggerations because his telling would enhance the herohood of all of them.

The hunt had one purpose over all others, to bring back food. A successful hunt meant survival for the hunters' immediate community, so the hunt was as far as one can imagine from today's hunting for sport, a take-it-or-leave-it affair. Hunting in those days was full of grave risk, to meet a great need, with success a life-and-death necessity for the folks back home.

The hunter was going after something he and his family or members of his clan needed. They needed it as soon as possible. And who knows the obstacles that had to be overcome. Perhaps the first animal the hunter tracked got away. Or perhaps the animal was huge and turned on the hunter, and it was the hunter who had to run away, but he still needed to bring back food, so he tracked another animal only to find a hunter from another tribe already carving up the carcass. Did they cooperate sweetly, or did they fight over the meat? Did the hunter who had killed the animal defend his kill successfully by hitting the other hunter on the head with a stone? I wasn't there. It's pure conjecture. But it demonstrates how the events of life may have led to the kind of stories that were first told over fires. There are heroes and villains, and always conflict over something, food, turf, belief, all the subjects that have been dealt with thousands of times since in fiction.

It would be useful for writers today to think of the hunt when planning stories. Is what the protagonist wants or needs a serious matter? Does getting it mean taking risks? Is success if not a life-or-death necessity at least a matter of some consequence?

The title of this chapter poses a question, "Is Conflict a Necessity?" Let's answer that right off. Yes, conflict was and is a necessity, it is the essence of dramatic action. The engine of fiction is somebody wanting something and going out to get it. And if you let him get it right away, you're killing the story. He can't get it because a mountain or a man is in the way, nature and human nature in opposition to achievement. Without that opposition, fiction is a vehicle without an engine.

Many people—including some inexperienced writers—bristle at the term "conflict" because of memories and overtones, and so I propose another term for their consideration, "adversarial." I would like to drive home the fact that the adversarial nature of fiction is not something that surfaces when protagonist and antagonist meet in battle. Successful writing is permeated with an adversarial spirit demonstrated in suspicion, opposition, confrontation, and refusal. The conflict is often verbal, not high drama, sometimes even mundane. I want to provide you at once with an example of how an ordinary exchange over a minor matter can be interesting because it is adversarial. We will go for our example to Richard Bausch, a short-story writer and novelist whose work has merited a Modern Library edition of his selected stories. In his story "Police Dreams," we find the following exchange between a wife waking a husband who has to wake his children:

> "Casey," she said.
> "I'm up," he told her.
> "Don't just say 'I'm up.' "
> "I am up," Casey said, "I've been up since five forty-five."
> "Well, good. Get *up* up."

That's what I mean by "adversarial." Our temptation is to write what we might say in life, "Casey, come on, get up." Take another look at how Bausch makes that simple plea interesting for the reader by a deft touch of opposition.

> "Casey," she said.
> "I'm up," he told her.
> "Don't just say 'I'm up.' "
> "I am up," Casey said, "I've been up since five forty-five."
> "Well, good. Get *up* up."

Adversarial doesn't mean the Battle of the Marne, or Good Guy locked in physical struggle against Bad Guy; it doesn't mean a shouting match any more than it means a fistfight. Adversarial exchanges are a key element of successful fiction, for without an adversarial pitch the same material might come across to the reader as boring. We must not confuse conflict that can be ruinous in life with conflict that is the essence of fiction. Readers enjoy conflict *because* it is in fiction and not in their lives.

It is easy to be confused by the need for physical as well as psychological opposition at a time when the movies exploit our senses with overloud soundtracks of shooting, burning, screaming, and the rest of action junk that only inures audiences to violence. If character A looks character B in the eye, and character B looks away, you have an adversarial action. If character A asks B a question, and B turns his back and walks away, you have an adversarial action. If the writer's characterization is good, when a mother tells the boy "No more cookies," and the reader knows the moment she is out of the room the boy will be at the cookie jar, you have an adversarial action. I am purposely advancing seemingly minor matters to emphasize the fact that the adversarial spirit of strong fiction often lies in the details of everyday life.

In childhood we are taught a lie: Sticks and stones will break my bones, but words will never harm me. Words can hurt. Some things said are unforgivable. Dialogue is one of the best means of sustaining the adversarial nature of strong fiction. Every audience that has heard me say "He loved her and she loved him and they lived happily ever after" knows how bland and boring the non-adversarial can be.

The stories that affect us as readers can deal with disappointment and loss, with small defeats and minor victories. Their emotional grip on us may be modest, but they help us understand each other. Historically, however, the stories that become part of the culture that is passed on to future generations for the most part deal with the evils of human nature for which there seem to be no remedies within our grasp. Oedipus slays his father, and gouges out his own eyes when he learns who it was that he killed. Hamlet kills Polonius behind the arras. Shakespeare, the man universally acclaimed as the greatest writer in any language, used deception, poison, torture, and murder, and is revered not only for his language but also for his candid, incisive, and accurate depictions of human nature.

Human nature is the real subject matter of all writers who take their work seriously. Despite the Enlightenment, human nature hasn't changed in the millennia since the first stories were dramatized. The twentieth century embroiled us in wars that killed tens of millions, a high proportion of them civilians, including children. As I write, only small clusters of those who survived the Holocaust are still alive as witnesses to what ostensibly civilized nations did to whole populations. The fratricide of Bosnians, Rwandans, Kosovars, and Serbs rocks our senses because we want to believe that human nature has improved since Cain slew Abel. We've killed prisoners of war with their hands raised. Torture unknown to animals is still practiced by man. Allegedly sane men blow up public buildings full of people innocent of any grievance that the bomber has. Humans unknown to the gunmen are shot in airports, or die in airplanes that are sabotaged, hijacked, or struck down by missiles. The human race is not nice, though some people are. Why not then write about nice things instead of conflict? Why have writers always added to the record of evil in the world?

Why does an auto accident attract an audience?

Why is bloody boxing considered a sport?

Is it because it is happening to someone else? As in books. Or on stage.

H. L. Mencken said, "The primary aim of the novel . . . is the representation of human beings at their follies and villainies, and no other art form clings to that aim so faithfully." Note that Mencken said "primary aim," not "sole aim." Similarly, I am not suggesting that novels should be about conflict exclusively. Love, compassion, the pleasure of children can be as compelling as their opposites, though perhaps not for Mencken, who was a brilliant sourpuss. Adventure, fantasy, wonder, the joy of discovery in nature or art or business, and an endless number of upbeat themes will continue to be the subjects of fine fiction. Each story, however, will require, as stories have since the beginning of time, a spine of conflict to quicken the reader's pulse. And adversarial exchanges will be there to lift dialogue off the printed page.

While conflict is a necessity, it is not a constant necessity. Any novel that strings together conflict after conflict will soon enough come across to the reader as a flatline on an EKG, a deadly sameness. The reader, weary from experiencing the characters' conflict, appreciates what even a soldier values, a few moments of rest. But the best writers know how to provoke the resting reader's curiosity, preparing him for the next clash.

In the manuscripts that come my way, the fault is seldom too much conflict. I am continually amazed by the number of writers who choose to dampen their stories with nonadversarial, static events that can change a page-turner into a ho-hummer. A writer has to look only to his own humanity to find the material for conflict. Is there a writer alive who has not envied? Who has not been intimidated, even momentarily, by an intellectually or physically more powerful adversary? Has he not quarreled with a neighbor even in his head, has he not ever experienced lust, fought with friends, lied to himself or others, and perpetrated illegal acts in his imagination? Were the Ten Commandments fashioned for the people of another planet, or for us?

Do any of the characters in your novel envy others, quarrel, lie, or imagine perpetrating illegal acts? There you have four of the many ways to create an adversarial sense. Whether or not the imaginative conflicts we create are therapeutic for readers I leave to others. The point is that all fictional writing since the beginning of time—plays, myths, legends, stories, novels—has involved the drama of conflict, dissent, opposition, with the conflict usually personified in a protagonist and an antagonist, a hero or heroine and a villain. The opposing force may be a group of people, but it is almost never as effective as the single antagonist. And yes, the opposing force may be the weather or some other element of nature, but that is far more difficult to write in a way that will hold an audience, unless a protagonist and an antagonist can humanize the conflict. Lenin, the father of Soviet barbarism, said it succinctly: *Who Whom?* If your stories lack sufficient conflict, perhaps those two words should be inscribed somewhere you will see them often.

The principle of giving an individual face to the antagonists in a conflict holds true even for nonfiction. A remarkable example is *Rising Tide* by John M. Barry, the story of the greatest natural disaster in America. In 1927, the Mississippi River flooded an area roughly equal to Connecticut, Massachusetts, New Hampshire, and Vermont combined. Water as deep as thirty feet covered acreage from Illinois and Missouri to the Gulf of Mexico. Thousands of people died. Nearly a million were left homeless. The Red Cross had to feed nearly seven hundred thousand refugees for months. Despite the enormity of the disaster, the drama of the book centers on two engineers, James Eads and Andrew Humphries, who became respectively the protagonist and antagonist of this award-winning book. Eads was one of the greatest engineers of his time, compared by some to Da Vinci and Thomas Edison. For flood protection, Eads believed the land along the Mississippi could be spared if outlets were provided for the river if it flooded. Humphries, Chief of the U.S. Army Corps of Engineers, favored levees to contain the great river. Humphries, who comes off as the villain of the book, won. When in 1927 the rains came to the Mississippi basin without letup, the rampaging river battered the levees. The levees broke, and the river engulfed a huge portion of the surrounding states, destroying lives and property. What sustains the experience of reading about that disaster is the conflict between two strong-willed engineers. It was nature against man, nonfiction and not invented, yet what holds the reader to the page is the *personalized* professional conflict between two influential men, each a fanatic in his belief in what would save the population from harm.

Some writers are attracted to the inner conflict within a person as the spine of their books, which is fine if dramatized in dialogue and action *within the context of an external conflict.* If the internal is the sole conflict, however, that may be one of the most difficult of all stories to hold the reader's attention for hours, and should be attempted only by the most experienced writers.

Numerous writers spoil their chances for publication by trying to avoid the essence of drama that has energized plays for millennia and fiction since the form took hold. Central to dramatic action is, of course, the clash of antagonists, a strong need thwarted by a personified antagonist. An old man ruminating about his better days is a bore. In Hemingway's *The Old Man and the Sea*, the old fisherman is out to prove that he can still hack it. His antagonist is a great fish, the reader experiences the struggle, and though the fish is a skeleton by the time he gets it to shore, the old man is triumphant.

The struggle needn't be between a specific man and another specific man (or fish). One of the great novels of the twentieth century is Franz Kafka's *The Trial.* In that book, a man called Joseph K. is arrested one morning on charges that are never made clear. He tries to find out what he is accused of. His antagonist is not a single person but the bureaucracy of the law, and in the end he loses his life. Bureaucracy exists in my village, and likely in yours. It is a pervasive enemy of common sense and fairness, promotes indolence and deceit, yet it seems there is nothing we can do about the behavior of petty officials who are the enemies of reason, and sometimes cruel in their effect. *The Trial* is an enthralling book to read because it is difficult to avoid seeing bureaucracy as a precursor of totalitarianism, in which the functionaries of the state are arrayed against the individual, who can do nothing to save himself. What makes the experience of reading *The Trial* frightening to the perceptive reader today is that bureaucracy is an evil that has outlived the totalitarianisms. The prisoner K. is up against all the bureaucrats who conspire against him in the name of some undefined order that ultimately takes his life. The book has become a classic because of the excellence of its writing and the importance of its theme, but let us not overlook the fact that the driving force of the novel is a man straining against opposition. The reader feels the enormity of his struggle, hopes for his vindication, and suffers his defeat. Without the conflict, *The Trial* might be a lesson in sociology, but it would not move us profoundly without the sense of a defining struggle.

Man against man, man against woman, man against fish, man against bureaucracy, all demonstrate that conflict, subtle or severe, is the motor that drives dramatic action. It is the life enforcer of fiction.

THREE

Capturing the Reader

We all know about love at first sight, the initial glimpse of a person whose attractiveness for us is special, perhaps even overwhelming. On further acquaintance that initial instinctive burst of feeling, becalmed, can bloom into a relationship that is less dramatic and longer lasting, and in some cases an enduring love that may last a lifetime. But we meet so many others who do not varoom our emotions instantly. We may like them, but we do not love them. I find the reactions of readers to books remarkably parallel to their reactions to people they meet. That includes the professional readers who use the expression "love" to approve and "don't love" to relegate books to a lesser category of experience.

The first person the writer is trying to attract is a prospective agent. How many times have I heard a top-ranking agent say, "I like that book, but I don't love it." That means they won't link their professional life to the author's. To sell a novel in a difficult market the agent has to feel that anyone who rejects this book is dead wrong. Conviction sustains, but at the end of the process there must be a sale. If the agent isn't fairly certain he can sell a book quickly, he will reach for another manuscript. I know an agent who once distinguished himself by selling a book after one hundred unsuccessful submissions. Loyal persistence, however admirable, is a costly process. That agent now won't take on a book unless he is convinced he can sell it fairly quickly for an advance of six figures. That may sound outrageous to an author, but think of it from the agent's point of view. It costs the agent time and money to talk to editors, to inquire about interests, to have photocopies made, to send manuscripts around by hand or otherwise. How many times can one repeat that effort without diminishing the agent's commission and morale to zero?

My obligation to writers is to convey the reality, and to have that reality serve as a goad to making a manuscript as irresistible—and saleable—as possible.

If the agent takes a book on, the next reader in line, the editor, is open to falling in love because that is his trade, looking at every possible manuscript as the one that this day, this week, this month, will turn him on, and that he will want to live with for the many months of convincing his colleagues, the press, and the world that this novel is worth cherishing. As he reads, he will be thinking, "Can we sell this book? Does it fit our list? Do we need another book like this? Will the marketing director see its possibilities? Will it enhance or hurt my standing in the company?" That may seem cold. A publishing company, however, is today like every other type of commercial venture, a vehicle for selling a product in a highly competitive market. Few other products compete with thousands of products that promise a similar satisfaction. That is especially the case with a novel. A book about how to fix a car may be a necessity for a mechanic, and the competition may be only a few established books, but a novel competes for the reader's affections with hundreds of current titles and thousands still in print. A particular novel is a necessity for no one until they get to love it. Its utility is entirely subjective.

If you find this discouraging, and if you hoped for immediate appreciation and success, then perhaps you need to rethink the vocation of writer. If you are a writer, not a person who wants to be known as a writer, nothing will stop you, not even the long, hard road to success, which I am trying to make easier by providing some of the information, insight, and techniques you will need. One of my students who paid close attention to learning craft recently sold a short novel for a third of a million dollars. Another recent client has a novel that has had at least eighty-five printings, and he still strives mightily to perfect his new work. Other writers I've worked with have had their books become annuities, producing income each year decades after their work was done. I still receive royalties twice a year for work I did in 1953.

Now let me take you to the final reader, the one who is asked to pay for the company of your book. Browsing in a bookstore, he surveys the possible choices, perhaps attracted by a jacket design, the familiar name of an author, or a book's closeness to his fingertips. He picks up a book. He may read the front flap of the jacket, and then read a page or two. At some point soon, usually in the first three pages, he will make the decision to take the newly attractive story home with him, or, if what the browser first reads isn't enticing, there are all those other books to turn to that one might—just possibly—love reading.

The verb "to love" may be hyperbole in the case of books, but how often we use it. When a friend says, "I love that book," it is the friend's recommendation to you to share that experience. And few things help a book to succeed more than the word of mouth of the earliest readers.

What is it that entices the reader in the first few paragraphs of a book? Most often it is a character one wants to get to know better. The reader can be curious about a compelling situation. The reader can be beguiled by the writer's voice, an amalgam of the many factors that distinguish a writer from all other writers, an attraction similar to finding someone's speaking voice engaging, the way they say things, the sound of the voice itself.

An enticing first paragraph will get a reader (agent, editor, book buyer) reading on. The first page, if the reader's attention is held, will lead to another page. Once the reader's curiosity is captured by a character or situation or the excellence of the writing, it will cause him to do what editors do, take the manuscript home, high on hope.

All of this is prologue to the need to fashion the opening of every novel so that the reader will want to take it home, to make those first moments count. You want—and need—to get that opening right. To that end, in this chapter we are going to examine together several quite different openings of novels that have been successful. We'll see, happily, the variety of ways one can quicken the reader's interest.

The first burden of the process rests on what fiction writers have learned to call the "narrative hook," whatever grabs the reader's attention and invokes his curiosity. Though, like other writers, I have used the term "narrative hook," my preference is to call the process the starting of the story's engine, the point at which the reader will not want to stop reading.

Writers are told that the hook has to come as close to the beginning as possible. I am not about to dispute that idea, but to expand it. Writers of thrillers and mysteries try to get the hook into the first paragraph. In mainstream fiction we have more time.

In novels that rely on melodrama rather than drama, and particularly in so-called thrillers, readers are now constantly assaulted by someone found dead in paragraph one of chapter one, or a bomb is about to go off, or a killing is about to happen. As the dangers of the real world escalate into acts of terrorism, thriller writers have had to balloon their plots and increase the dangers. But if it is true that the reader must know the people in the car before he sees the car crash, many thrillers don't give us that opportunity. Readers may have some curiosity evoked, but the depth of their emotions is untouched by the kind of cliched opening that starts with an unmotivated bang to unknown characters. There are notable exceptions. Toni Morrison, winner of the Nobel Prize for literature, starts *Paradise* with "They shoot the white girl first." That's melodrama, but no reader expects Toni Morrison to write a thriller, and they'll gladly wait to find out who the people are.

And so we have a choice. You can begin with a flash fire in the kitchen that endangers the entire house (melodrama), or you put a pot on the boil, bubbling and simmering, as you show your characters acting in a situation that is slowly alarming, a conflict developing into the big event that will hold the reader curious, concerned, perhaps even enthralled, gripped as if glued to your story for its duration.

Anna Quindlen is the author of bestselling novels that draw remarks from reviewers such as "compassionate" and "tender." Her novel *One True Thing* is an example of drawing the reader into the writer's world. The first sentence of the Preface is intriguing: "Jail is not as bad as you might imagine." The reader imagines jail is awful, so he wants to know why the narrator thinks otherwise.

> When I say jail, I don't mean prison. Prison is the kind of place you see in old movies or public television documentaries, those enormous gray places with guard towers at each corner and curly strips of razor wire going round and round like a loop-the-loop atop the high fence. Prison is where they hit the bars with metal spoons, plan insurrection in the yard,

> and take the smallest boy—the one in on a first offense—into the shower room, while the guards pretend not to look and leave him to find his own way out, blood trickling palely, crimson mixed with milky white, down the backs of his hairless thighs, the shadows at the backs of his eyes changed forever.
>
> Or at least that's what I've always imagined prison was like.
>
> Jail was not like that a bit, or at least not the jail in Montgomery County. It was two small rooms, both together no bigger than my old attic bedroom in my parents' house, and they did have bars, but they closed by hand, not with the clang of the electric, the remote controlled, the impregnable. An Andy Griffith jail. A Jimmy Stewart jail.

At this point, the reader is ready to accept that the character is in an easygoing jail. The author, working backstage as it were, goes on making it seem that the jail cell is "not really unpleasant." But now the as-yet-unnamed first-person narrator (we learn only later that it is a woman, young at the time of this scene) is feeling alone, but also "peaceful as I could not remember feeling for a long time. And free, too. Free in jail."

What's going on here? From the narrator's thoughts we learn some things about her parents. The mother uses a wheelchair. The living room has been rearranged so her mother can sleep there. The couch has been disfigured in a way that lets us understand that the mother is very sick.

The police officer minding the jail comes by.

> I had seen him last at the town Christmas-tree lighting ceremony in December, when my mother's tree was the nicest tree, with its gaudy decorations and big red bows. He had

> been on the high school basketball team and had sat out every game.

The reader is being given a sense of ordinariness, but he wants to know *why is the narrator in jail?* Only after several pages do we find out that this young woman who feels so free is "a girl charged with killing her own mother." The engine of the story suddenly revs up.

> At the end I always did what she asked, even though I hated it. I was tired to death of the sour smell of her body and the straw of her hair in the brush and the bedpan and the basin and the pills that kept her from crying out, from twisting and turning like the trout do on the banks of the Montgomery River when you've lifted them on the end of the sharp hook and their gills flare in mortal agitation.
>
> I tried to do it all without screaming, without shouting. "I am dying with you." But she knew it; she felt. It was one of many reasons why she would lie on the living-room couch and weep without making a sound, the tears giving her gray-yellow skin, tight across her bones, the sheen of the polished cotton she used for slipcovers or the old lampshades she painted with flowers for my bedroom. I tried to make her comfortable, to do what she wanted. All but that one last time.

We are now convinced that she killed her mother against her mother's wishes. We are at the last paragraph of the preface:

> No matter what the police and the district attorney said, no matter what the papers wrote, no matter what people believed

> then and still believe, these years later, the truth is that I did not kill my mother. I only wished I had.

Hey! The reader's curiosity is high. Did she or did she not kill her mother? We've learned a lot about the town, the imprisoned girl's family, we have been sucked into the life of the community, and we are about to get to chapter one of the novel. What we have experienced is not the one-sentence or one-paragraph hook of pot-boilers, but a careful, slow spinning of a web. Anna Quindlen is manipulating the curiosity of the reader, pricking the reader with multiple surprises, making him read on.

Readers enjoy surprise. Surprise alerts the reader to the notion that this novel could be fun to read. Notice how it was done by Wally Lamb in his first novel, *She's Come Undone*:

> In one of my earliest memories, my mother and I are on the front porch of our rented Carter Avenue house watching two delivery men carry our brand-new television set up the steps. I'm excited because I've heard about but never seen television. The men are wearing work clothes the same color as the box they're hefting between them. Like the crabs at Fisherman's Cover, they ascend the cement stairs sideways. Here's the undependable part: my visual memory stubbornly insists that these men are President Eisenhower and Vice President Nixon.

Lamb's book was one of the most successful first novels of its time. The narrator would seem to be a child (we soon learn the child, a girl, was then four years old). The vocabulary of a four-year-old is limited. The perception of a child is mixed into the telling. If the author had confined himself to what a four-year-old understood, he couldn't have gotten very far. So we have an adult describing how something was perceived by a child. This double perception—adult as child—provides the fun. Notice the precise details with which the author continues.

> Inside the house, the glass-fronted cube is uncrated and lifted high onto its pedestal. "Careful, now," my mother says, in spite of herself; she is not the type to tell other people their business, men particularly. We stand watching as the two delivery men do things to the set. Then President Eisenhower says to me, "Okay, girlie, twist this button." My mother nods permission and I approach. "Like this," he says, and I feel, simultaneously, his calloused hand on my hand and, between my fingers, the turning plastic knob, like one of the checkers in my father's checker set. (Sometimes when my father's voice gets too loud at my mother, I go out to the parlor and put a checker in my mouth—suck it, passing my tongue over the grooved edge.) Now, I hear and feel the machine snap on. There's a hissing sound, voices inside the box. "Dolores, look!" my mother says. A star appears at the center of the green glass face. It grows outward and becomes two at a kitchen table, the owners of the voices. I begin to cry. Who shrank these? Are they alive? Real? It's 1956; I'm four years old. This isn't what I've expected. The two men and my mother smile at my fright, delight in it. Or else, they're sympathetic and consoling. My memory of that day is, like television itself, sharp and clear but unreliable.

What a crazy mix! The business of the checker in the mouth is clearly the perception of a young child. When the two show up on the TV set, the narrator refers to "the owners" of the voices, a child's perception. But the rest seems to be narrated by the child as an adult, and this mix continues as the story itself gets going in the paragraph that follows. An obsessively strict critic would point to the mix of ages in the narrator's perception as a flaw. But strict adherence to rules can set limits to the imagination. Wally Lamb tried the mix, and it worked for millions of readers who were fascinated and decided to let this unusual form of storytelling into their lives.

In the case of *She's Come Undone*, the surprise (Eisenhower and Nixon as the deliverymen) and the mixed child-adult perception may have intrigued the reader first. The engine of the story starts in the third paragraph, when we learn that the TV set was a gift from Mrs. Masicotte, a rich widow who has some kind of mysterious relationship with the narrator's father.

In three paragraphs the reader has met the four-year-old girl, her mother, and now the "other woman." The reader's curiosity has been aroused not only about the character of the narrator with the mixed voice but also about the relationship of the benefactor, Mrs. Masicotte, to her father. The engine is turning. The story is going somewhere. The reader wants to go on.

You don't have to find a body in the first sentence, or blow up a stadium, to prickle the reader's hairline about what might happen. It may be easier to sell a novel today that starts with a bang, but the bang has to be credible, and has to mean something to a character the reader can quickly care about.

The tug at the reader's lapel can be a matter as small as a man who doesn't care much about eating and his wife who cares too much. Here is the beginning of *The Stone Diaries* by Carol Shields, which won the Pulitzer Prize for fiction in 1995 and became a national bestseller:

> My mother's name was Mercy Stone Goodwill. She was only thirty years old when she took sick, a boiling hot day, standing there in her back kitchen, making a Malvern pudding for her husband's supper. A cookery book lay open on the table: "Take some slices of stale bread," the recipe said, "and one pint of currants; half a pint of raspberries; four ounces of sugar; some sweet cream if available." Of course she's divided the recipe in half, there being just the two of them, and what with the scarcity of currants, and Cuyler (my father) being a dainty eater. A pick-and-nibble fellow, she calls him, able to take his food or leave it.
>
> It shames her how little the man eats, diddling his spoon around in his dish, perhaps raising his eyes once or twice to send her one of his shy, appreciative glances across the table, but never taking a second helping, just leaving it all for her to finish up—pulling his hand through the air with that dreamy gesture of his that urges her on. And smiling all the while, his daft tender-faced look. What did food mean to a working man like himself? A bother, a distraction, perhaps even a kind of price that had to be paid in order to remain upright and breathing.
>
> Well, it was a different story for her, for my mother. Eating was as close to heaven as my mother ever came.

What are the characteristics of this slow opening that might intrigue the casual reader who hasn't heard about the book? The narrator is telling us about her mother and father, using one focus, their greatly different attitudes toward food. We may be reminded of a nursery rhyme: "Jack Spratt could eat no fat, his wife could eat no lean." Something else may intrigue the reader, the way the father is characterized, "raising his eyes once or twice to send her one of his shy, appreciative glances across the table," or "his daft tender-faced look." What's going on between them? Soon enough we learn that the mother is a mountain of flesh from overeating, and this little man does have an appetite, not for food but for his wife's buxom body. And so page by page the narrator feeds us small particularities that make this couple, this family come alive.

You can also build a beginning with a setting, including a particular setting's place and time in history. Building tension slowly is harder than the conventional accretion of thriller-type suspense in the opening paragraphs, the unidentified body found, the enemy preparing to blow up God-knows-what, or an in-your-face threat to the protagonist who is not yet a beloved character. In *The Magician* I started the first chapter with *deceptive* calm.

> It had been snowing off and on since Christmas. For nearly a month now, while the men of the town were at work, boys would come out in twos or threes with shovels to clear a pathway on their neighbors' sidewalks. An occasional older man, impoverished or proud, could be seen daring death with a shovel in hand, clearing steps so that one could get in and out of the house, or using a small snow-blower on a driveway in the hope of getting his wife to the supermarket and back before the next snow fell.
>
> At night mostly, when the traffic had thinned, the town's orange snowplows would come scraping down the roads, their headlamps casting funnels of still-falling snow. Alongside these thoroughfares, the snow lay in hillocks, some ten or fifteen feet high, thawing a bit each day in bright sun, then refreezing, forming the crust on which it would soon snow again. It seemed impossible that spring might come, and that these humped gray masses would eventually vanish as water into the heel-hard ground.

Of course, it was beautiful to those who looked up at the huge evergreens dusted with snow, and above them the bare webs of leafless silver maples reflecting sunlight. In the fields at the outskirts of town, one could see, after twenty-nine days of snow, half-mile stretches of the untrampled season's glory.

Young children enjoyed the marvelous fluff to tramp in or throw, but to their elders in the village of Ossining, the snow was nature's trick, daily defeating the salt spreaders, snowplows, calcium chloride, studded tires, and the hopeless attempts to get rid of the garbage stuffed into cans outside the back door. The food scraps and containers crammed into huge plastic bags and other makeshifts alongside the overstuffed cans testified that through a month of relentless snowfall, human consumption continued day after day.

Unlike the neighboring village of Briarcliff Manor, which was almost entirely middle-class, and the small section called Scarborough, which was upper-middle-class, Ossining also had working-class neighborhoods, and a large black slum.

Located in the richest county in the United States, Ossining itself was not at all rich. Though Ossining had the highest tax rate in the county, the center of the village had numerous empty storefronts; nearby homes were run down, fled from. The biggest drain on taxes was, of course, the schools, in which violence was not unknown. Working-class family cars, like gunboats, displayed the flag. Parents suffered their children who succumbed to long hair. It was not an unusual town in a country on the decline after two centuries.

Ossining had originally been named Sing Sing, after the Sinq Sinq Indians who inhabited the area from the Pocantico River to the Croton. But long before Hollywood made Sing Sing prison known throughout the world, the local inhabitants divorced themselves nominally from the men behind the walls and changed the name of their village to Ossining. The state eventually caused the prison to be renamed the Ossining Correctional Facility, but the townspeople did not have the will for a further change of name. They accepted it as they did all-numeral telephones, the inefficiency of public servants, the dearth of honest craftsmen, and the lack of a place you could take a car to be repaired by a good mechanic. It wasn't the end of the world.

In Ossining this January day, an extraordinary young man of sixteen named Edward Japhet was practicing magic tricks in front of a large mirror in his parents' bedroom. . . .

The detail is designed to lend an ominous overcast to the scene before the action of chapter one begins. The town is enveloped in winter. An older man is daring death with a shovel in hand. It seems impossible that spring might come. We hear of class and race division in the town. We see numerous empty storefronts, homes fled from. There are hints of violence in the schools. It was not an unusual town in a country on the decline after only two centuries. And then the reader comes upon the village's name, Ossining, the home of Sing Sing prison. It is only on the third page of the novel that the reader meets the protagonist, sixteen-year-old Ed Japhet, the magician. I trusted the quiet omens to light the reader's curiosity about the place before I introduced the character. It turned out to be a risk worth taking, though introducing a character doing something interesting is a safer way of starting.

We are about to plunge into the subject of keeping the reader reading by examining two quite different openings of novels I know well because I edited them, and that demonstrate the variety of means available to engage the reader.

The book we will start with was a turning point in both the author's career and mine. *The Arrangement* by Elia Kazan had a compulsive quality for many readers. Nearly a million people bought it in hardcover. As I indicated earlier, it was number one for thirty-seven consecutive weeks. Let's try to understand why. This is the way the book begins:

> I still haven't figured out my accident.
>
> I've gone over and over the events of that day, the day of the crash, with all the hindsight I've gained in the years since. I've gone over the events of the months leading up to the crash, the events that should account for it. But there is still a mystery.
>
> The riddle is not that a man as successful as I was would try to kill himself. There were reasons why I might have. I had everything, as they say, but still there were reasons. The mystery is in the way it happened.
>
> I don't believe in ghosts. But even today, when I'm a totally different man and live in a totally different way, when I ask myself exactly what happened, I next ask myself what hand and whose it was that reached in out of the absolute blue, jerked the wheel of my Triumph two-seater around, and, despite all my strength and all my will, held the course that plastered me against the side of a speeding trailer truck. It all happened in a short second or two, but that is what I distinctly remember.
>
> Success ought to provide some protection against ghosts or the unconscious or whatever it was. That is the least you should be able to expect of success. Or of money. But they didn't, either one. I found myself helpless—I'll say it again—against the strength of that "hand" or whatever it was that

wrenched the control of my Triumph TR 4 out of my grip, held it unswervingly on course, and finally packed it against the side of that trailer truck.

The events leading up to my accident don't tell the reasons. True, eleven months before, I had given up a girl to whom I was very attached. But I had righted myself during those months; in fact I was doing great. My wife Florence and I were the envy of every other married couple in Beverly Hills and Bradshaw Park. The Golden Couple! That nickname was awarded us during those very eleven months between the day I gave up Gwen and the day of my accident. Besides, most of the men I know have faced a similar painful choice at some time in their lives—made it and in time recovered, feeling deprived perhaps, but much sounder.

And I knew I had to give Gwen up. I knew the moment was on me, that moment when you can still walk away free and clear, without lasting injury to either side, and just before that other moment when somebody's going to get hurt. I had a pretty damned good idea of the danger I was running; in fact I had said to myself again and again, "Walk away, kid, before it's too late!"

I had asked myself the basic questions. I mean if you're with a woman twenty-one years as I had been with Florence, there is something of value there. And not to mince words, divorces are costly things. I didn't even really know this other girl, or to speak the truth, I knew one side of her very well: every little flesh pad and pocket.

But hell, I thought, I have too much to lose. I mean I was an established man, then; I was solvent, set for life. I owned this beautiful house in the Bradshaw Park section of Los Angeles, and I had there (this will seem absurd, I know) the

> goddamnedest lawn in that whole area, and some wonderful plantings that I had put in myself, and a really great record collection, including many rare 78's; two valuable Picasso original drawings; a deep freeze that held thirty-six cubic feet of food; and the three cars: Florence's continental, my daughter Ellen's Karman Ghia, and the Triumph TR 4 which I was later to smash up. All that and a swimming pool. It was a lot to give up for a good lay, or even a great one! And when I looked at all that stuff and my family too, I thought what the hell am I getting into? Every man will know just what I mean, especially Europeans, who despite general impression are much less romantic than we are and really understand property.

When *The Arrangement* was first published, Alex Haley said, "This book has got a motor in it." He proved to be absolutely right. An interesting thing happened to me as I was typing the above excerpt. I was impelled to keep going, to provide more, which I take to be roughly equivalent to the reader's experience of wanting to know more.

With the passage of time, there are several things in the book that seem old-fashioned. An attractive young woman is called a "girl," the practice of the time. There is some repetition. Some sentences are not quite grammatical. None of that seems important. What was it that you, as a reader, *wanted to know*? That is what's important.

If the first-person narrator is not what we call "a nice person," what redeeming feature does he have?

What is at stake for the narrator? Do you care?

If you've answered for yourself, compare your answers with mine. We don't necessarily have to agree. What we're trying to determine is why so many readers were attracted.

What I want to know is why did the accident happen? Was he trying to commit suicide? Over what?

A few paragraphs after the excerpt we learn how good the narrator's wife, Florence, had been to him when they first met.

> I loved Florence. . . . our bond was close. We'd met when I was at college, and ever since then she'd been my good magic. I was a mess when she met me, crouched down in my little burrow, my legs drawn up under me, ready to spring and snap, teeth bared and ready, eyes frantic. She was the first one who dared reach down to me. She coaxed and eased me up and out of my solitary hole. It took time, and I snapped at her gentle patrician hand a few times—more than a few times. But she persisted and finally managed it. Then she set about straightening me out of my crouch, or was it a cringe, the posture I'd been in all my life.
>
> Florence had seen something in me no one else had. Just the way she looked at me—I remember the testimony of her eyes in my favor the first time she left those eyes open for me to look down into, the first time I really saw them unveiled, soft and warm in a face of English pink. I remember other things about her then, too: her hair, how it was combed and brushed. She looked at me in those first days, and she didn't have to say, "Believe me—" or "I'm telling you the truth—" like most people have to. She just had to look at me and I knew she believed in my worth, whether anyone else did or not, and that she loved me, whether I did her or not, and that she was mine forever, whether I wanted her or not, no questions asked.

This woman Florence made it possible for the narrator to have his pride and to succeed, to assemble the wealth he now had and was ready to throw overboard for the sake of a younger woman. Clearly a cad. Why is the reader held?

Eddie's redeeming feature is his candor. He seems utterly frank about his faults. He is vulnerable. *Both of these characteristics help a reader believe in a character's reality.* Take that thought back to your own manuscript. Is your protagonist, male or female, candid and vulnerable? If you look back at twentieth-century novels you have liked particularly, you'll find a common denominator in the candor of their protagonists, especially if the story is told in the first person. And the vulnerability of a protagonist is now a given. We no longer believe in perfect heroes and heroines and completely villainous antagonists. We are attracted to the humanity of both when they are credible, and because they are like us when we are being honest about ourselves. If your character comes to lifelikeness quickly, the reader won't let go.

I have said many times that a writer writes what other people only think. The author of these extracts, Elia Kazan, had the courage of candor. As candid an author as Henry Miller called Kazan's "a great book. When you touch it you touch a man." The initial reception by women, perhaps surprisingly, was equally strong. Eleanor Perry, reviewing the novel for *Life* magazine, said, "By the end of the book, Elia Kazan has achieved what is most needed on this shaky planet—a new working model of a human being. . . . This is a novel to change your life by." With endorsements that strong, it is easier to see why the book shot up the bestseller lists. Its title, *The Arrangement*, coined a meaning that is now in our vocabularies.

Let's examine the next book by the same author, *The Assassins*, and see if you detect in the opening the ingredients that attracted readers.

> They were flying out the next morning, and Master Sergeant Cesario Flores had a farewell word to say. He did this cor-

rectly, as he did everything else, saying neither too much nor too little, singling out no one for praise or for censure. He allowed they were a good troop and if he heard some day that they were really doing a job, he wouldn't be surprised. He reminded them for the hundredth time that the men flying the planes could be no better than the maintenance on the ground. Then he said the word, "Goodbye," paused, seemed to be thinking, pushed his sightly tinted glasses up to a more comfortable rest. His last joke was a postscript; he didn't expect to hear from any of them personally, but if he did, please no more dirty oriental postcards, he'd had enough from the last gang he'd trained. When he smiled you could see he was Mexican, de las Flores.

The men laughed and whispered; then they saw he was waiting for them to be silent. When they were, he said, "You're representing a great country, don't forget that!" He seemed about to add something caustic, didn't. That was it. He walked up to the men, twenty-seven of them, shook hands with each, calling him by name and rank. It was as close as Sergeant Flores could come to giving them his blessing.

The bulky body turned, correctly and in place, the sergeant picked up his hat and walked out of the shop, down the clapboard-lined corridor to the exit, out and under a sign which read, THROUGH THESE PORTALS PASS THE PRETTIEST MECHANICS IN THE WORLD, past another the sergeant himself had ordered, PRIDE, and so to the first parking slot at the side of the building, the one with his name painted on the macadam. His car was a Dodge, GI brown, and belonged to the air force. Sergeant Flores checked the rearview mirror to see that it was correctly an-

> gled, cinched his seat belt though he was only going three hundred yards to the office of his commanding officer, Colonel Francis Dowd.

This opening doesn't have the same immediacy as the opening of Kazan's previous book, with the first-person protagonist questioning the reason he swung his car into a suicidal crash. What we have in this opening is a master sergeant saying good-bye to a group of soldiers he has just trained. What about this beginning might conceivably interest a reader?

A cynical but correct answer might be that the reader had read or at least heard about the huge success of the author's previous book and was curious about what he'd do this time. Maybe it was the book's title, *The Assassins.* Or the flap copy, which proclaimed this a book that takes place during an era of assassinations, of ritual murder, of the killing of students by police and of the police by assailants who kill without warning, and of the boys who drop death by airplane in far places. But that isn't fair. Judge your interest by the text alone; that is all I saw before the manuscript became a book.

The sergeant is delivering a quite ordinary farewell to the troops he trained. The first paragraph ends, "When he smiled you could see he was Mexican, de las Flores." All in all, a nice guy. He talks like a patriot. He pays attention to each individual among his trainees. He is giving them his blessing. At the end of the quoted passage, he's off to see his commanding officer, but that doesn't come across as foreboding. What do we have here?

This nice guy, Cesario de las Flores, is going to murder someone. We don't know that yet, but the title of the book haunts us. Why is it called *The Assassins*?

The beginning is subtle. In the subsequent paragraphs we get the sergeant's background, how he married overseas, the kind of woman his wife is, and his care for his daughters, particularly the older one.

> Elsa [Cesario's wife], of course, complained that Cesario hopelessly spoiled their eldest. At seventeen, Juana still sat on her father's knee, there got anything she wanted, an Indian princess stranded on an air base in the middle of a desert in a foreign land.
>
> For Cesario, Juana was the only part of Mexico left to him. He couldn't stop fussing with her. In town he'd walk up to a complete stranger and ask where she'd bought something she was wearing, a blouse, a skirt, an ornament. The woman might, at first, think he was getting fresh, but then she'd look at Cesario's earnest face, the heavy anxious eyes behind the tinted glasses, that bulk of innocence, and she'd listen while he explained why what she had on would look good on his daughter and please, no offense, where had she bought it? That night the item would be on Juana.

It is Juana's boyfriend that the sergeant will murder.

In many conventional novels, the murderer comes across as evil. Here, the reader is lured by the seeming ordinariness of this career soldier, this nice guy, and when we learn of his upset, we understand his anger, and then *he does something awful that seems understandable under the circumstances we have already experienced*, we live through his trial *on his side*.

Let us remember that the author's job is to manipulate the reader's emotions. Because of the title, *The Assassins*, we expect violence, but we don't expect the violence to come from Cesario. As the pages go by, the reader gets uneasy, he doesn't want Cesario to do anything rash, but Cesario, motivated, does it anyway, and that leads to further violence and the theme of the book.

We've just examined two openings of novels by Elia Kazan that intrigue readers through the characters and their concerns. We can learn more about the creation of characters by seeing how he created the character of himself for his autobiography. Though the following is nonfiction, it is hardly different from the way an interesting novel might begin:

> "Why are you mad?"
>
> My wife asks me that, seems like every morning. Usually at breakfast, when my face is still wrinkled from sleep.
>
> "I'm not mad," I say. "It's just my face."
>
> I've said that to her ten times. She's my third wife and I'm happy with her, but she has yet to learn that I don't talk in the morning. Which is tough on her, a decent person, full of lively chatter, like bright pebbles.
>
> Confronting me where I'm sitting at my typewriter is a small round mirror, clamped in a pretty but rickety Mex-made stand. It frames my face neatly, and sometimes when I work, I study my image. I certainly look mad.
>
> The fact is I *am* mad, most every morning. I wake up mad. Still.
>
> "Haven't you noticed that everyone is afraid of you?" My wife goes on, her tone gentle and sympathetic. "You're intimidating."
>
> "Bullshit!"
>
> "Ask your children. Or mine." She's brought me two blond stepchildren, nice kids. "They're scared of you too."

I'm rather good at concealing anger. Had to be in my old profession. But recently it's begun to show through. What I'm mad at nowadays is, for instance, mortality. I've passed seventy-eight and have only recently found how to enjoy life. For one thing, I've stopped worrying about what people think of me—or so I like to believe. I used to spend most of my time straining to be a nice guy so people would like me. Now I'm out of show business and I've become my true grumpy self.

I no longer hid it; it's out in the open, my perennial scowl. Which is why my smile, when it does appear, is so dazzling. The sheer surprise of it! That's supposed to be a joke.

Sometimes the image I see in the little round mirror shocks me. There he is—my father. I'm beginning to look like the man I feared most of my life and particularly during the years when I was growing up. I look away. I look back. He's still there, and his face still disturbs me.

To involve the reader's attention, the author has isolated one part of his anatomy, his face. He has presented it in an adversarial context, his wife complaining about his face. And we find out where he thinks that face came from, his father, and we are into the story of his life. In fact that's what he calls the book, *A Life*, and in my judgment it is one of the few great autobiographies of the century, more candid than any I can recall, and full of examples that will profit any writer who studies them.

There's an interesting exercise you might try. Like Kazan, isolate one thing from your own life, not necessarily your anatomy. It could be a habit of dress, a gesture, an idiosyncrasy, even a kind of oddball thought that passes through your mind on occasion. Take that one thing and play it like a fugue, elaborate on it the way Kazan did about his face. Just try a half page in which you talk about the one thing, be as candid as you can, and as unlike anyone else you know in your choice of characteristic. Let your imagination go. When finished, you can keep it for your own autobiography, or better still, use it to characterize somebody important early in your novel. The character will appreciate it. And so may your readers.

FOUR

Success Lies in Seeing the Details

Early in Russell Banks's novel *The Sweet Hereafter* a school-bus crash triggers the story. The reader will know about the accident from the flaps on the book jacket or the paragraph on the back of the paperback. It is important for the credibility of the accident that the school bus and its driver be as real as possible for the reader. Six or seven pages into the book, we find the following two paragraphs of detail:

> My first stop that morning was at the top of Bartlett Hill Road, where it branches into Avalanche Road and McNeil. I pulled over and made my turnaround so the bus was facing east and waited for the Lamston kids to come down the hill on McNeil. The three of them, since the day the oldest, Harold, started school, always got to the stop late, no matter how often I threatened to leave them if they weren't there waiting for me, so eventually I just made it a habit to come a little early and pour myself a cup of coffee and wait. It's like when they were born their clocks were set permanently

five minutes behind everybody else's, so the only way you could meet them on time was to set your own clock five minutes early.

I didn't mind. It gave me a chance to enjoy my second cup of coffee in solitude in the bus with the heater running. It was peaceful, way up there on top of Bartlett Hill looking west toward Giant and Noonmark and Wolfe Jaw, watching the sky lighten, with the mountains outlined in black against this milky strip of light widening from the horizon. Made you appreciate living here, instead of some milder place, where I suppose life comes somewhat easier. Down in the valley, you could see the house lights of Sam Dent coming on one by one, and along Routes 9 and 73 the headlights of a few cars flashed like fireflies as people headed out to work.

An inexperienced writer might simply say the driver of the school bus was waiting, as usual, for the three Lamston children, who were always five minutes late, but that wouldn't be writerly. Russell Banks has it this way:

> It's like when they were born their clocks were set permanently five minutes behind everybody else's, so the only way you could meet them on time was to set your own clock five minutes early.

Similarly, an inexperienced writer might say that down in the valley you could see the house lights of Sam Dent and the headlights of a few cars. Note Banks's use of particularity:

> Down in the valley, you could see the house lights of Sam Dent coming on one by one, and along Routes 9 and 73 the

headlights of a few cars flashed like fireflies as people headed out to work.

"Writerly" is a good word we ought to use more often. It refers to the kind of writing you expect and value from a writer who takes his work seriously, who uses detail to create lifelikeness. Conversely, you wouldn't expect to find writerly expressions often in business or academic writing, though I've seen it in both on rare occasions. I have two friends who are high-ranking judges and who like to get a writerly expression into their decisions or other writings. Writerly expressions give pleasure to the person who invents them and to the reader who encounters them.

Let's look at some other examples. For instance, a layman might say, "Clothes don't make the man," which is a cliche. A writer might freshen the idea with "the important creases are in the brain, not in the pants."

Writerly expressions use detail to particularize. "There is a kind of thought that sticks in your head the way a piece of chewing gum can stick to the sole of your shoe. The more you try to get rid of it, the worse it seems to get." The ordinary way of conveying something similar is "Some thoughts are hard to get rid of." Note that the latter is in general terms, while the writerly version uses a particular detail, a comparison with chewing gum stuck on the bottom of a shoe. Writerly writing employs simile, metaphor, and, most important, detail, preferably visual detail that is fresh.

Once a writer makes a habit of trying to phrase what he thinks in a writerly way, even his everyday communications will begin to show traces of writerliness. When the habit sticks, the writer may not notice that a phrase he has written is writerly until he reads it again at a later time. For instance, on the phone with a fellow writer, I said, "The light at the end of the tunnel is a man with a flashlight yelling, 'Go back!' " In casual conversation, it was a reflex without conscious thought.

The writer owes it to the reader to be amusing, entertaining, interesting. Writerly expressions contribute mightily to the reader's pleasure. I've noticed that novels deficient in such matters as suspense, plot, and even characterization have managed to interest readers *solely because of the writer's skill with words.* Writerliness is important for all but transient fiction, and even those popular novels that depend primarily on suspense and plot have been better received both by reviewers and readers when the author's words were fresh, specific, and detailed.

In the decades of the Cold War, readers were deluged with spy fiction, much of it highly forgettable. However, David Cornwell, who writes under the name John le Carré, has had a spectacular career in large measure because his spy stories are writerly. Georges Simenon, an amazingly successful writer of mysteries, won reader loyalty in many languages, and particularly from his French audience, which appreciates the writerly use of language. At one point Simenon said, "I consider myself an impressionist because I work by little touches. I believe a ray of sun on a nose is as important as a deep thought." Maybe yes, maybe not, but Simenon had a successful career because he noticed distinctive details.

John Steinbeck's novels do not have the reputation of being especially literary, despite his Nobel Prize for literature. Yet he was choosy about words. "They can change their meanings right in front of you," he said. "They pick up flavors and odors like butter in a refrigerator."

I see manuscripts and books that are spoiled for the literate reader because they are one long stream of top-of-the-head writing, a writer telling a story without concern for precision or freshness in the use of language. Some of this storytelling reads as if it were spoken rather than written, stuffed with tired images that pop into the writer's head because they are so familiar. The top of the head is fit for growing hair, but not for generating fine prose. Cliches cross our mind because we've used and heard them many times. In conversation we have the habit of using cliches to communicate facts ("It's raining cats and dogs outside") or to say how we feel ("I've been under the weather since I got up this morning"). The casual conversations of writers good and bad are littered with cliches. It takes a conscious effort for the writer to get away from top-of-the-head expressions in his writing.

Our education sometimes doesn't help produce good writing. Careless writing is tolerated by teachers of subjects other than writing. I felt lucky that my two youngest children had the benefit of a school whose headmaster insisted that no student pass a subject unless they could write about that subject in clear, uncluttered English. Even in classes where so-called composition is taught, some teachers focus on grammar and punctuation, which is fine, but neglect the creative uses of language, which is not fine. Students are asked to write an essay about what they did over the summer vacation, telling rather than showing, with no conscious attempt to evoke the experience in the reader. They are sometimes told to put down detail, but no mention is made of fresh detail. They are not stimulated to think of similes or to create metaphors. They are taught to communicate but not to evoke. They are not taught to be writerly in their writing. That's a lot for the victims of careless education to overcome if later on they develop an interest in writing stories for others to read.

Fortunately, some children have an ear for language. With the stimulation that comes from wide reading, they learn the pleasure of artful, accurate images. Some sense on their own that good writing does not consist of first thoughts written and never revised. Some demonstrate a natural gift for fresh observation, of a young imagination let loose to explore. But how few students are actually taught that creative writing is created for a purpose, that purpose being the pleasure of the reader, and that there are techniques for creating that pleasure.

T. S. Eliot had a fancy phrase for what evokes emotional experience in the reader. He called it the "objective correlative," a term heard by decades of students but understood by few. Part of the blame rests with Eliot, for his definition is murky. He said, "The only way of expressing emotion in the form of art is by finding an 'objective correlative'; in other words, a set of objects, a situation, a chain of events which shall be the formula of that particular emotion." Eliot trips over "expressing emotion." The writer's job is not to express but to create an emotion in the reader. And what I believe Eliot meant by that obfuscating phrase "objective correlative" is a fresh detail or an action that will create an emotion in the reader. Let's look at an example intended for that purpose.

In a work-in-progress, a high-ranking executive is about to make a decision that will have a profound effect on his life. I needed a "beat," a few seconds delay to slow the story down before the day of decision gets going. My object was to have the reader feel the beat, the pause before the decision is made, and for the pause to have some meaning.

> Early the next morning, as Amory headed for the garage, his special oak tree, the one that marked the end of the lawn, let go of a leaf. It drifted one way, then the other, losing altitude, wafting like a slow pendulum till it settled, brown and intact, on the pebbles at his feet. He stooped to pick it up by the stem. Against the early morning light, he could see every vein of its astounding symmetry. As he laid it carefully on his left palm, wondering what to do with it, the dry leaf fractured into crumbs, its shape vanished. He let the remains drop to

the hard ground. For an insane second he wanted to stoop and salvage one piece of it to put in his wallet.

He looked up. The oak had plenty of leaves left. He got into his car and zoomed out of the driveway, headed for the great restorer, work.

Ten readers will have ten differing reactions to that passage, but the emotion of those readers should be alike, a momentary relaxation of tension, a moment of peace and contemplation, and then off to the office, where the important decision will be made and the story erupts.

Mark Twain, who loved to chide other writers, needs a little chiding himself. He once said, "What is the real function, the essential function, the supreme function of language? Isn't it merely to convey ideas and emotions?"

Twain is on the right track, then veers. The supreme function of nonfiction is to convey facts as well as ideas. In fiction, the supreme function is not to convey emotions but *to create them in the reader.* And the clue to creating them is fresh detail, which Mark Twain supplied in abundance. The writer, as craftsman, does not necessarily feel what he wants his reader to feel. Stephen King doesn't need to be terrified to create a feeling of momentary terror in his readers.

Newcomers to fiction writing have asked me how they could develop an eye for detail. It is a matter of focusing, as you would with a camera. The French film director Henri-Georges Clouzot created tension in an interrogation scene by focusing on a hand pulling on an earlobe, a foot tapping. Some writers focus on detail instinctively. Others can develop the habit of observation. For instance, take a walk with a friend. Before you start, suggest that you each try to remember as much as you can of what you see on that walk. You are not to point out anything to each other. At the conclusion of your walk, ask your friend to tell you what he or she remembers of what they saw on the walk. If your friend is not a writer, he will in all likelihood come up with large objects, a brown house with white shutters, a line of poplar trees, a shallow stream rushing over rocks. What a writer with an instinct or training for observation is likely to come up with are particular details that are out of the ordinary, the overturned garbage pail alongside the brown house with white shutters. The writer might notice one poplar tree that had many of its leaves missing, perhaps some bare branches, a tree dying. Or given the regimented appearance of a row of poplar trees, the writer might see them as a line of tall green soldiers guarding the edge of the property. Or at the shallow stream, the writer might have noticed the largest of the rocks jutting out of the water, a hazard to adventurous boaters, a protector of the stream from human interlopers. Or the one shredded shoelace in his companion's right sneaker that is begging to be replaced. Detail is the salt that enriches what the eyes see. Focus, then let your imagination loose.

You don't need to take walks with a friend to exercise your skill in observing detail. Stare at any object until your imagination transforms it from what it is into *what it might be*: a lonely tricycle at the side of the house, still hoping to become a bicycle because its owner had grown up so quickly.

If no object within sight stimulates your imagination (there should be!), flip open a dictionary and look at the first noun on the page. How can you make it interesting? As I wrote this, I opened my dictionary, and the first noun I saw was a tough one, "goiter." But a few seconds' thought gave me "the goiter looked like a package of wobbly fat that some enemy had stuffed under his handsome face." You can get both characterization and a sense of story by trusting your imagination.

In a restaurant, even when I'm having dinner with the best of companions, I can't help but be rude because I'm taking in the other people within sight: the young woman straining to seem elegant rather than starched, and her companion, a shy boy hiding behind a red-dotted bow tie between his Adam's apple and the rest of the world. Some people don't like being stared at. Be a camera that clicks and looks away, and if you need more detail, wait a minute, then turn back to the person and click again. Sometimes a detail is worth jotting down, with an apology to my dinner companion, who knows that I'm a writer and that I'm rudely doing research all the time.

I don't want to leave the subject of detail without a reminder of the reason it has become increasingly important. The earliest storytellers could tell their tales in general terms. During the eighteenth and nineteenth centuries, with fiction newly disseminated in books, stories and novels used narrative summary a good deal. In narrative summary, you will recall, offstage actions are reported to the reader, told rather than shown. Today, the reader who has no special interest in literature and reads for enjoyment of the experience usually finds discomfort in novels that use mainly narrative summaries to recount what happened offstage out of the reader's sight and hearing, events told about rather than witnessed.

It is important to understand the reason for the reader's discomfort. There has been a drastic change in storytelling in the twentieth century, and the reason for that change is unfortunately not usually taught in schools. Writers need reminding that we've all had exposure to movies, a visual medium, and for half a century a massive exposure to television, also a visual medium. Today's readers have learned to see stories happening before their eyes. They tend to skim or skip long passages of description or narrative summary. If you're looking to get a book published in today's world, there's no point in writing for dead audiences. As writers, we need to be aware of and appreciate the fiction of previous centuries, but we have an obligation (to ourselves) to keep in mind that we are writing for living audiences who have preferences characteristic of our time.

Animals rely most on their acute ability to smell or hear. Their vision is poor compared to humans'. Vision is mankind's most important sense. As writers, our interest in visual detail is a response to the most acute sense we have. We term the showing of events as they happen in front of the reader "immediate scenes." One way to be sure that you are writing an immediate scene is the film test. If a scene is not filmable, it is not immediate.

The emphasis on immediate scenes is new, but it is not new to the art of story. Long before there were novels, there were plays, and that durable art consists almost entirely of immediate scenes. The difference between most plays and today's fiction is that when we see a play on stage, we see characters full length and a massive amount of their surroundings. In most innovative theater, however, the sets are not realistic. One or two pieces of furniture and a picture hanging in space against a black backdrop may represent a living room. The author or set designer or director has selected what we are to see. The rest is supplied by our imaginations. Similarly, in fiction the best novels do not give us laundry lists of clothing worn by the characters, and paragraphs of description for a setting. In each case, the writers employ particularity, choosing which significant detail characterizes best. The reader is perfectly capable of filling in the rest. You need to depict an ill-fitting jacket, not a whole suit. You need a character's eyes that look everywhere except at the speaker, not a whole face.

Experimental writers sometimes neglect what the reader can see, limiting their audience unnecessarily. Writers of so-called commercial fiction sometimes muck up visual scenes because they show action inaccurately. And both kinds of writers—particularly those who have never written for the stage or film—often lapse into narration, unaware of what they are doing. They are not conscious of trying to appeal to the reader's eye. A writer who wants to be read by contemporary audiences—the only ones available right now—and possibly by audiences of the future, will find it useful to study through example the differences between narrative summary and immediate scene. Keep in mind that narrative summary is telling and immediate scene is showing. Also keep in mind that almost any offstage event can be brought before the reader's eyes, a technique described in *Stein on Writing*.

It is easy to be nostalgic for the past, when writing was more leisurely. John Barth in his masterful *The Sot-Weed Factor* and John Fowles in *The French Lieutenant's Woman* have produced innovative books touched with irony and complexity that perceive the past with a contemporary vision. I admire the work of both authors, their talent, and their daring. But for the writer of fiction who has not yet published or not yet published well, and who wants to be published successfully, neither narrative summary not drastic experimentation is the most practical route to first publication. Fowles started out with a much simpler contemporary novel called *The Collector*, about a young man who falls in love with a girl, kidnaps her, and holds her hostage. It was an instant success and established a reputation for Fowles that enabled him to go on to more-experimental work. James Joyce did not begin with *Ulysses*; he mastered short stories first.

We crawl before we walk. When I first learned to walk, I couldn't turn around and change my direction without falling. When I was blocked by a wall or furniture, I'm told, I sat down, turned around while sitting, then got up and walked some more. It was not very efficient, nor greatly experimental, but it got me where I was going. Just as later I learned to turn around while standing, the writer needs to build on his abilities and strengths before trying fancy maneuvers. Know the molds you break. Picasso did not start out being Picasso.

Above all, remember that generalities are blurry, and that precise detail is what enables the reader to see—and experience—your scenes.

FIVE

Characters Who Are Characters

You and I are sitting at a small table outdoors at a sidewalk café in Paris, watching the people stroll by. I invite you to play a game. Pick any passing pedestrian you see in time for me to notice him. Or her. I bet you'd choose someone who was oddly dressed, or walked in an unusual manner, or was carrying something bizarre. One notices people who stand out in a crowd. That is exactly the kind of character you want for your novel.

The surviving novels of the twentieth century, different as they may be from each other, have something important in common. Their protagonists are eccentric. Think of Holden Caulfield in *The Catcher in the Rye*, Henderson in Saul Bellow's *Henderson the Rain King*, Jay Gatsby in *The Great Gatsby.* In Faulkner's novels, nearly all the characters are eccentric. A reader can be seduced by character. It is interesting that a number of writers, detecting some value in eccentricity, have created eccentric characters out of themselves. The reclusive author of *The Catcher in the Rye*, J. D. Salinger, turned himself into a conspicuous hider, one hopes more for privacy than publicity. Tom Wolfe's new novel, *A Man in Full*, is number one on the bestseller list as I write. Tom Wolfe, with his three-piece white suit and hat, created an eccentric character, himself, and that drew attention to his journalism and then his novels.

In the end, it is the eccentricity of the characters in the novels that helps them endure. If we go back to the novels of the nineteenth century, we have Captain Ahab in *Moby-Dick*, Mark Twain's Huckleberry Finn, Raskolnikov in Dostoevsky's *Crime and Punishment.* Many of Dickens's important characters are eccentric. Why all the emphasis on characters who are out of the ordinary, who often have fierce desires, strange mannerisms, and unrelenting drive? Readers don't want to pay money in order to spend twelve hours in the company of someone who is just like their neighbor next door. They are attracted by differentness. These eccentricities are not what holds the reader. Readers identify with the main character's humanity, hopes, temptations, joys, triumphs, vulnerability, and sadness.

We're still sitting at the sidewalk café. You've made a few notes about the character you've picked. I now ask you, "What does that character want?" Whatever your answer, my response would be, "That isn't enough!" I'd prompt you to imagine something bigger, more immediately important, to open your mind to the possibilities your imagination could generate. I might hint that it would be more interesting if your character wanted something badly, and wanted it now. While you're thinking, at an opportune moment I'd suddenly ask, "What do you want that's more important than what that character wants?"

If you were to blush, I'd be glad. If you took your time, I'd goad you for an answer. If you came up with the kind of top-of-the-head things that writers sometimes blurt out—fame, bestsellerdom, a movie sale—I'd dismiss those desires because so many writers want the same things. I'm prospecting for your special, perhaps secret desire that's been the subject of fleeting thoughts you've brushed aside. If we're in luck, you might come up with a longing of yours that would be ideal for the eccentric character in your book. If your hero wanted what you want badly and didn't get it, if your hero encountered obstacle after obstacle and you figured out ways for him to overcome them one by one, you'd be plotting not only from character but at least partially from your own store of feeling, from some yearning that could become the foundation of a story you could write with fervor. In our not-yet-acknowledged secret garden lie the seeds of some of our best not-yet-written stories.

I am tempted to tell you two incidents from life. I once knew a successful writer who was conspicuously attentive to his wife. He'd rush across a room with a chair if he thought she wanted to sit down. He'd try to anticipate her every whim. One day his wife disappeared. This devoted husband expended his waking energies for weeks searching for her. He located her thousands of miles away, living under primitive circumstances with an aging hippie who looked as if much time had passed since his last bath. From what I had observed about the lives of this couple for years, I concluded the wife was sending the husband a strong and as it turned out final message. His constant exertions to be so conspicuously kind, sweet, nice, attentive, to be the nicest nice guy imaginable, had made him predictable and boring to the point where she had to flee. What she fled to was as different as possible from the life she had previously led.

Cliches, the tired expressions writers try to avoid, are frequently based on a truth. Nice guys finish last. Whether or not that's true, nice guys, male or female, are totally unsuitable as the protagonists of fiction. I know because when I finished my best-known book, *The Magician*, the manuscript was handed back to me by my wife,

Patricia Day, a professional editor, who said the main character, a sixteen-year-old boy named Ed Japhet, was a goody-goody, a flat character who spoiled a novel that was otherwise alive. I was a volatile individual in those days, and I don't remember if my first impulse was to destroy myself or take it out on the editor. I slunk away, and when calm descended, I reexamined my novel. The lady was right. I wasn't a nice guy, why did I make the young magician a nice guy? I revised an early scene in which Ed Japhet is unwinding just before leaving his house with his magic equipment to give a performance at his high school. The fact that Ed's father is a teacher at the school is an embarrassment to them both. The following exchange was added:

> His father, seeing no light under the door, came in on tiptoe. He turned on the small desk light rather than the overhead in order not to startle him.
>
> "I thought you might have fallen asleep."
>
> "No," said Ed, "just resting."
>
> "I feel awkward about this."
>
> "About what?" said Ed, raising himself from the bed.
>
> "Well," said Mr. Japhet, "I'd like to see the show."
>
> "You've seen all these tricks."
>
> "It's just that it's different in front of an audience." Mr. Japhet examined his fingernails. "I mean, if you were playing football, you wouldn't mind my coming to the games."
>
> "That's different."
>
> "How?"
>
> "All a player sees is the crowd. When I do a show, I see people's faces. In fact, I fix on one or two and talk to them. If you were there, I'd see yours, and it'd make me nervous."
>
> "Doesn't Lila's being there make you nervous?"

"She's going to sit way in the back."

"I could sit back there, too."

"Oh, Dad, the prom isn't for parents."

The reader feels the father's pain and wishes Ed would let his father see the show. After Ed is attacked by the leader of a school gang, and the gang leader is arrested and put on trial, Ed refuses to cooperate with the justice system because he doesn't believe in it. Ed is no longer a "nice guy." Additions of this sort made all the difference. Everything good happened to that book, over a million copies were sold, it was selected by the Book-of-the-Month Club, was widely adopted by high schools, had many foreign translations, and enjoyed a long life in print, which I attribute to giving an overly "nice" kid some faults.

To be accepted by the reader, your main character has to come alive, and what energizes protagonists is their zeal, their desire, and their ability to do some things extraordinarily well. To seem real, they must be vulnerable in some respect. Most fiction writers know that. Some writers find it difficult to give their main players characteristics we think of as bad, meaning aggressive, impatient, selfish, rude, bossy, immodest. We notice one or more of those characteristics in people we love, then fail to give any of them to characters we want our readers to love. I learned that lesson through another character in *The Magician*, George Thomassy, who has now inhabited five of my novels, and who is anything but a nice guy. Thomassy is a lawyer who is out to win no matter what. He is not nice to district attorneys. He intimidates a witness to keep her from appearing in court. He's a forty-four-year-old bachelor who sometimes poaches on other men's women. After Thomassy appeared in *Other People*, my publisher kept track of the women who wrote letters offering to marry him!

One of the ways in which I built the character of Thomassy in

Other People was to let the reader witness scenes from the past. The reader sees Thomassy getting his first sex instruction as a boy from his father, an Armenian immigrant trainer of horses. The reader witnesses a quarrel between father and son when Thomassy announces his intention to become a lawyer instead of a horse trainer like his father. The father is especially angry that Thomassy has changed his name from Thomassian.

I even took the reader to a layer of life beyond the father, to the old country during the Turkish massacre of the Armenians in 1915. In other words, I gave Thomassy dimension by giving him a family with a history in a novel that is happening in the present. The reader senses how Thomassy became the man he is, spectacular in his field, charming when he wants to be, yet a man riddled with moral flaws characteristic of tough litigators. That's what I mean by growing a character, giving him a history in a way that is embedded seamlessly in the present story. The reader accepts this not-nice guy as a fighter who will take nothing less than winning at any cost, and cheers him on. What is important is that the character comes to life. Years after the book's publication, at a large party in my house, I observed a group of lawyers and judges discussing how Thomassy would handle a certain case that was in the news—as if he were alive.

Many years ago a literary agent sent me a nonfiction manuscript by Jimmy Hoffa, the notorious longtime head of the Teamsters Union. The manuscript was actually written by a ghostwriter from audiotapes made by Hoffa during a series of interviews. Hoffa had had a colorful life, but the manuscript was pretty blah. I asked to borrow the tapes to authenticate the material. The tapes were colorful, pure Hoffa, tough and real. The writer had "cleaned him up," made him into a nice guy. I suggested a lunch meeting. On the appointed date, Hoffa arrived at the publishing company's headquarters with his agent, the ghost's agent, and an entourage of his associates, men who looked out for Hoffa's well-being. My editors were all eager to meet Mr. Bad.

Let me characterize Hoffa for you as if he were a character in a book. When he arrived at the headquarters of Stein and Day Publishers, a three-story historic mansion called Scarborough House in suburban New York, I came out to greet Hoffa and his entourage. Hoffa seemed a bit ill at ease. I suppose he had never met a publisher before. My custom was to give first-time visitors a tour of the place. I led the way up the stairs to the editorial floor with Hoffa at my side and his entourage following. We were halfway up, when Hoffa suddenly elbowed me in the side. Without thinking, I elbowed him back. On the second floor I introduced Hoffa to several of the editors who would be accompanying us later to lunch. Next, we were on our way up to the third floor, where the business offices were located. There was a spectacular triangle-shaped seventy-foot-wide window up there from which one could see the Hudson River and a vast expanse of greenery.

Halfway up the second flight of stairs, Hoffa again elbowed me and got an elbow back, at which point he laughed, and turning to his entourage, said, "Hey, this publisher is all right." He based his judgment on the fact that when he elbowed me, I elbowed him in return. It seemed to make him feel more comfortable in an environment that was new to him. Hoffa's elbowing was the kind of particularity that characterized him the way I would ask you to choose a particularity to characterize your protagonist.

The mistake many writers make is to present a slew of characteristics, when one that is just right would do the job much more efficiently. In the case of Hoffa, the characteristic was an action, something trivial on the surface but important to the character, testing the person he was about to get involved with, in this case a different species, a publisher! And it was something you as the reader could see. Notice that I didn't stop the story—the tour of the premises—to present the characteristic.

We proceeded to lunch at Dudley's, a nearby restaurant of local fame. Present around the table were Hoffa, his advisors, and several of my editors, who, from earlier comments, were all expecting to dislike Hoffa because he had the reputation of being a tough, street-smart ex-convict. At lunch, Hoffa surprised them—and me. He was charming, not like Cary Grant but like Jimmy Hoffa, who had been admired by millions of truck drivers for whom there was no other.

Amidst this geniality, I had a message to deliver. I suggested to Hoffa and the agents that for the book to be acceptable they had to restore the voice of the tapes, the sometimes foul language, the tough comments, even the grammatical errors. The cleaned-up version of the manuscript, I said, wouldn't interest readers and therefore wouldn't interest me. We shook hands all around. I suppose everybody was happy except the ghostwriter, who fortunately was not present. Thirty days later Hoffa went missing, and in a record four days fifty thousand hardcover copies of the book rolled off the presses on the way to bookstores. What I remember most about the meeting was the unusual gesture that characterized Hoffa, and how he charmed the group of editors. Hoffa was a character fit for fiction.

One of my criticisms of most thrillers that come my way is the lack of compassion the reader feels for the heroes and villains alike. It won't do for the author to tell us he has compassion for a character, it has to be conveyed by an action, something the reader sees and feels. What was there in Hoffa's manuscript that made me feel for him?

Hoffa lived in a street-tough world where violence was not unknown. As a young truck driver and union organizer, he carried a piece of pipe in the cab of his truck for protection. What raised my compassion was an incident when he was first courting Josephine, who became his wife of many years. Early in their relationship, young Hoffa pulled up his car at the curb in front of her house and honked his horn for her. Her parents were shocked, and wouldn't let her come out to him. In his background, honking a horn outside was apparently okay as a way of summoning someone, but in Josephine's background, it was déclassé. He didn't know that. I felt compassion for him because the occasion was so important and, out of ignorance, he failed. Matters like that, seemingly small, are useful to the writer who wants to create compassion in the reader.

Sherlock Holmes became a much-beloved character. His drug addiction worried his friend Dr. Watson. Watson is critical of Holmes's habit, but does not condemn him for it. The reader wishes Holmes could abstain, and knows he can't. This feeling toward the undesirable habit of another person is one of the many means a writer can use to help the reader feel compassion.

Compassion is also closely related to a certain tension produced in the reader of fiction when a character is in serious, perhaps irremediable trouble. With skill the reader can be made to feel compassion even for a character he hardly knows. John le Carré had two early novels that weren't especially successful. Then *The Spy Who Came in from the Cold* was launched. In the first chapter of the book, the narrator is waiting for a colleague to escape from East Germany over a bridge. The reader sees the man coming over on a bicycle. He is noticed by the East German guards. The reader has been set up to want desperately for the man to escape. The tension is great, and when the man is shot, the reader feels dismay at the death of this unknown character who has failed to make it across.

It is not death that in itself evokes the reader's feeling. In most mysteries and thrillers a body is found early, but only in the most carefully crafted fiction does the author set the reader up to feel the death. In the movie world's action thrillers, the viewer becomes so inured to mayhem on a large scale that the killing of a human being does not touch the compassion of anyone watching. There is something immoral about witnessing a death without feeling it. The thoughtful writer should care for his characters in a way that would make any threat to them, any suffering, something the reader would not want to happen, and to suffer when it does happen. That's the principal difference between characters that seem made up, who act to move the plot forward, and characters who come to life, which is precious and which the reader must want to preserve.

To hook the reader, many writers put a death right smack in the opening before the reader can feel anything. The death feels told. What le Carré did in *The Spy Who Came in from the Cold* is to have the character who is killed be on what the reader realizes is an important mission. The reader cheers the character on. Escape is near. The reader hopes all will be well before, suddenly, the escape fails and the reader is moved.

Is there anything you can do to stimulate your muse if a character you're working on seems flat, lifeless, conventional? Earlier we've seen how a little contretemps between Ed Japhet and his father helped bring life to a flat character. If you're finding it difficult to give a character color, pick up a children's book, preferably in a library or bookstore where lots of children's books are at hand. If there's one book that affected your emotions as a child, steep yourself in it again. If not, just browse. You'll meet characters more extravagant than those you'll usually find in adult fiction. After you've exposed yourself to half a dozen colorful characters, go back to your character and see what you can do to replace his or her ordinariness with characteristics that are fresh and wild like those that frequently inhabit children's books.

If that doesn't work for you, try this. Take the "ordinary" character that you're trying to improve, and look in his pocket. Find something that would surprise him greatly. What is it? How did it get there? Does it embarrass him? Is it something he wishes he had not found? How can he get rid of it? If he puts it somewhere, will someone observe him and bring the object to him as something he left behind? The first character to appear in my novel *Other People* was an upscale Wall Street lawyer, Archibald Widmer, father of the female protagonist. He says he "reluctantly perceived that civil and well-educated people now accept gratuitous violence against strangers as ordinary." That's just the kind of fusty character who might seem flat, except for his fear in the first paragraph that the protections are gone. His twenty-seven-year-old daughter has been raped by someone who lives in the same building his daughter lives in. The father, we learn in time, carries in his wallet a snapshot of his daughter in the nude. With that the reader's perception of him as a fusty, old-fashioned lawyer is superseded by the image of a vulnerable man with a secret. Any character with a credible, interesting secret has a good chance of coming alive.

Why not write down the four words of the title of this chapter someplace where you'll see them often when you're writing: Characters who are characters.

SIX

Backstage: Where Writers Get Their Plots

I don't want to pick a quarrel with my writer friends who make a large distinction between story and plot. I think of story as the *idea* or *conception*, as in "this is a story about . . ." Plot is the working out of that idea in scenes that can be changed, shifted about, added to, or deleted. In literary fiction, the story develops from a character, or the idea for the story triggers the development of the principal character. The idea becomes "a story about so-and-so, who . . ." In transient fiction, characters are often created to fit the story idea. An exception is the series novels that have the same central character for each. The experienced writer of either literary novels or entertainments, once he has the conception worked out, should be dealing with *how to show the story in scenes.*

The essence of the story should be reduced to writing in as few sentences as possible. One sentence is better than two, two are better than three. In book publishing we call this the handle, which will later be used by the publisher's salesmen and publicists to describe the book quickly. The handle of *The Best Revenge* is "A successful Broadway play producer with a production in serious trouble, deserted by his usual backers, has to call on a new style of moneylender—a gangster nouveau—for financing. The play producer and the moneylender start out as the worst of enemies and in the course of producing the play end up the best of friends." If a shorter handle were required, the last sentence could be used on its own. A snapshot summary does not do justice to a complex book, but a handle is necessary for the publishing process. If the author doesn't come up with a suitable handle, someone on the publisher's staff will do it. If the author creates the handle early, it has the extra benefit of helping him design the plot.

In Hollywood, the story conception is trivialized as a "high concept," meaning an even briefer summary of the story. Skip Press, the author of the *Writer's Guide to Hollywood Producers, Directors, and Screenwriter's Agents*, refers to the high concept notion as "art reduced to twenty-five words or less." In the the film business, a so-called high concept is frequently a butting together of two existing successes, such as *National Lampoon's Love Boat.* In fiction, thankfully, the story idea is often related to something the writer has experienced or cares about deeply. A theme germinates. Within that theme, a character surfaces. The character wants something, but there are obstacles, and the story is off and running. How does this chain get started? How does one tap into the wellsprings of one's life and fish up a story idea worth spending years writing? And how does keeping a plot simple help a novel succeed in the marketplace?

I can speak for myself and for some of the writers I've worked with closely. The writer reaches into his memory for a person or event that left a heavy-duty marker that might just be ready for inspection. Elia Kazan's *America America*, now a classic, is a case in point. Kazan was four years old when his Greek parents emigrated to America in 1913. The original name of Kazan's family was Kazanjoglou, an attempt to add a Turkish gloss to a Greek name because life was hazardous for Christian Greeks living under

Muslim rule in Turkey. Though the United States was spoken of as a nation of immigrants, over the decades the idea of immigration became suffused with sentimentality. The actuality was different. Getting to America was usually fraught with anxiety, difficulty, and sometimes terror. Reaching the port of embarkation, and getting together enough money to pay for passage, were often a prolonged nightmare of successive defeats. Crossing the ocean in steerage was a tough trip. Good people sometimes did bad things to get to the promised land.

Kazan, by 1962 a distinguished director of movies and plays, hit on the theme of immigration, derived, he said, mainly from the experience of an uncle. He conceived it first as a screenplay (and later made a classic movie of it). Laymen find reading screenplays very difficult, and published screenplays don't sell very well. My job as editor was to turn the screenplay into fictional form so that it could be read with pleasure, retaining Kazan's highly individual, stark style and language without adding any words of my own. It took four drafts, but became a model for other screenplay conversions.

In the evolution of Kazan's story, an early step was to personify the story of immigration in a character who would become the protagonist. Kazan invented young Stavros, a twenty-year-old who was determined to get to America at any cost. Stavros worked almost literally like an animal, a *hamal* carrying great weights on his back, to earn money for the voyage. Kazan imagined many adversities for his protagonist, worst of all a bandit named Abdul, who pretended to befriend Stavros, then stole the money Stavros had put away. Stavros is fiercely willful, determined. Not even the sudden prospect of marriage to a rich man's daughter can deflect him from his goal of reaching America. Stavros will, in fact, commit a murder in order to achieve his goal. The story has the mythic force of a crusade. S. N. Behrman, the distinguished author of plays and essays, in his introduction to *America America*, said, "Mr. Kazan's style is Biblical in its simplicity and emotional intensity."

Let's recap the process of inventing a plot. The idea of *America America* was touched off by Kazan's family experience. It was developed around a character with a profound desire and an unstoppable intention to realize his goal. Plotting the scenes involved the development of obstacles, overcoming them, and finally, in a bittersweet ending, Stavros achieving his goal. The brief novel is full of strong scenes and memorable particularities. Its essence is a story that is clear and strong.

The reading public responded. The book, Kazan's first, sold over three million copies in bookstore and book club editions, and was widely reprinted in other languages in the countries from which America derived its population. Because Kazan was an accomplished film director when he wrote it, much of the book is strikingly visual. In its time it was recognized as the best work of fiction on the most indigenous American theme, immigration. In this day of short memories and the quick remaindering of history, a writer might wisely spend an hour or two in a library with *America America* and release himself to its grip. It is a wonderful example of fundamental plotting.

Another example of plotting strongly related to the author's experience is *Matador* by Barnaby Conrad. It is the story of Pacote, a great bullfighter past his prime, who is going into the ring against the black bulls one more time. Pacote fears that he will disgrace himself before the young upstart who is fighting with him, and before the crowd that has immortalized him. The plot is simple. The reader is pleading with the character, *Please don't go into the ring again, retire in full glory*, but Pacote goes into the ring, the reader witnesses a great bullfighting scene, and Pacote and the bull kill each other. The story is direct, simple, and moving, and is based on the career of Manolete, one of the great bullfighters of all time. *Matador*'s link to the author's experience is direct. Barnaby Conrad, San Francisco born, a Yale graduate, was posted to Spain as an American vice consul. There he studied bullfighting, and performed in the ring as the "California Kid." He drew on his bullfighting experience to write this elemental novel that is worth studying for the simplicity of its plot and how much it moves the reader. In 1952 *Matador* was a runaway, selected by the Book-of-the-Month Club and reviewed on the front page of *The New York Times Book Review*. It remained on the national bestseller lists for fifty weeks, sold three million copies, and was translated into twenty-eight languages. In the most recent edition (Capra Press), Conrad includes an afterword about the writing of *Matador* that details the origins of the story and provides some valuable insight for the reader who is also a writer.

The source of a plot can sometimes lead a writer to a character, or more accurately to what a character does. Like many boys at the age of twelve, I got interested in magic. I performed for events in my high school and did shows for pay. I wrote two nonfiction books on magic as a teenager, and in the armed forces toured as the magician in a show called *Chez Fatigue* before going off to Europe and serving in the occupation of Germany as a too-young company commander in the 1st U.S. Infantry Division. In Europe, I forgot about magic, but it didn't forget about me. When I came home, I tried to resign from the New York Ring of the International Brotherhood of Magicians. Instead, they made me an honorary life member, which prevented me from resigning ever. When I turned to writing novels, it was natural for me think first of a protagonist who was a teenage magician in high school. That's how Ed Japhet, the young protagonist of *The Magician*, was born.

Ed wanted to be let alone by the gang that ran an extortion racket in his high school. To personalize the antagonist, I created the character of Urek, the leader of the gang that demanded a quarter a week from each student to leave their lockers unmolested. Ed refused to pay the extortion money. After Ed's magic show at a school dance, Urek and his gang beat up Ed and his girlfriend severely. Urek is arrested for assault. The lawyer I invented to defend Urek proved to be a lucky break that caused me to change not the plot but the original idea. This was to be a book about two magicians, the teenage Ed Japhet, and the lawyer, George Thomassy, who performed his tricks in the courtroom. Thomassy successfully defended the gang leader, Urek. In the shift of the book's conception, the story became the one for which the book is now known, that justice in a court of law is an illusion in which the guilty can be held innocent. At the end of *The Magician*, Ed accidentally kills Urek in self-defense. Someone who kills in self-defense is still subject to trial. Ed, the boy magician, turns to the dead villain's lawyer, George Thomassy the courtroom magician, to defend him.

The Magician is a straightforward, elemental story that took off from the author's experience as a boy magician. It proved to be my most successful book. *The Magician*, like *America America*, supports the idea that in the early stages of developing a story, *it pays to root the story in an experience that was an important emotional marker in your life.* The writer has to create some distance from his own experience to gain the advantage of objectivity. Kazan used his uncle's experience, but transformed it. I started with a sixteen-year-old magician and ended with a lawyer who was a magician in the courtroom. Readers liked the lawyer character so much, I used him in four additional novels.

All three books I've mentioned so far are character-driven and strongly realistic. Let's now examine a recent novel by a student of mine that is far from realistic, a morality tale that turns on a concept relating to the author's profound spiritual belief. Before turning to fiction, Jerry B. Jenkins coauthored a good many celebrity nonfiction books. The concept of Jenkins's novel, *'Twas the Night Before*, is timely in an age when belief in angels is widespread and there is a tidal wave of concern with spiritual matters. This short novel was marked by a sale to a major book-publishing firm for a several-hundred-thousand-dollar advance.

The story of Jenkins's novel is elemental. Noella, a journalism professor at Northwestern University, and Tom, a reporter for the *Chicago Tribune*, are engaged to be married. When Noella insists that a medallion she received as a child is actually from Santa Claus, Tom's disbelief convinces Noella that they are just too dissimilar to marry. Tom, devastated by the breakup, flies to Germany to write a piece about the Father Christmas tradition. In Europe, a light plane he is in with five others crashes. The others are killed. Tom, injured, loses consciousness on and off, and has a mystical experience, with elves taking him to Santa Claus's workshop. He wakes up in a Swiss hospital and cannot answer how he got there to the satisfaction of the authorities. As a result of the accident, the lovers are reunited, but Tom, who now believes in Santa Claus and has a medallion to prove it, finds that Noella has lost her belief. Finally, when Noella's faith is restored, she and Tom are married.

The plot is a morality tale expressing belief in the unprovable, a fairy tale for adults. That's exactly the point of its inclusion here. Jerry Jenkins is a devout Christian, and this tale derives from his belief in the unprovable. His novel, *'Twas the Night Before*, subtitled *A Love Story*, has been compared to O. Henry's *Gift of the Magi* and Dickens's *Christmas Carol.*

Let's turn to a writer whose commercially successful novels tend to be plot driven. Their "morality" consists of us versus them, the good guys against the bad guys—the workhorse concept that has driven countless movies and books. Jack Higgins has published a novel a year for as long as I can remember. He writes thrillers, the best known of which is *The Eagle Has Landed.* His career is an object lesson to the would-be commercial or popular thriller writer. He had twenty-four books published before he hit it big with *Eagle.* I edited and published seven of his novels after *Eagle*, and we established a close working relationship, though his home was on the island of Jersey off the coast of France. Higgins disliked hotels. Whenever I'd be editing one of his novels or coaching him for his next publicity tour, Jack Higgins was my houseguest. The nearby village of Ossining is home to Sing Sing, the prison that the movies made famous. The warden of Sing Sing at the time was a fan of Higgins's books, which helped me wangle a tour of the inside. This wasn't a tourist tour. Sing Sing's inmates don't get sent there for traffic violations.

First we were shown through the minimum-security wing, which is wide open, with partitions instead of walls, prisoners ambling around, talking to each other or watching the communal television set at one end. No bars, no cells, more like a dormitory that the occupants are not free to leave. It was the place prisoners were sent who were due for parole or about to complete their served time, to give them a taste of freedom and prepare them for the outside. The authorities skipped showing us the medium-security section, and took us from the clubhouse atmosphere of the nearly discharged to a wing that was a world apart, locked barred door after locked barred door, a maximum-security cell block. We were ushered inside. To our surprise, the inmates were all roaming out of their cells. Higgins and I suddenly heard a clang behind us. We'd been locked in with the prisoners!

We had to assume the authorities showing us around thought of it as a practical joke. The prisoners glared at us. They had no idea who we were. Some muttered phrases I can't repeat here. Suddenly our attention was drawn to a huge prisoner on the upper level who was thumping down the metal stairway, carrying what looked like a glass milk bottle filled with water. Higgins froze. His immediate thought was that the burly prisoner would break the head off the bottle and use it to hold him hostage.

After a few frightening seconds, we heard the metal door behind us open, and guards motioned us out of the cell block to safety. Higgins was, of course, worth millions (his earnings averaged about two million dollars a book for the seven that I published), but the prisoners didn't know who he was or that he was rich. The hostage idea was his instant thriller-writer's reaction to what he, surrounded by prisoners out of their cells, perceived as the threat of the glass bottle. The flash of impending danger was over in seconds, as the door behind us was opened for our retreat. But let us imagine that Higgins would use the experience to develop a story: the celebrity visitor held hostage by the inmate with shards of a glass bottle.

I've related this true episode as a demonstration of the "what if" factor that is so important. It's how a writer's imagination might take advantage of what happens to him in life. The writer has a lot of leeway, of course. Instead of an imaginary walk through a prison cell block when the prisoners are out of their cells, the writer could focus on one of the characters, the bully, the snitch, the educated accountant who's living among the people he always thought of as on the other side of the tracks, the innocent convict who had a lousy lawyer. The chosen inmate might even be the protagonist. The experience Higgins had, in the hands of different writers, would lead to different stories. You might say, "Wait a minute. I don't get to visit places like Sing Sing for inspiration." I would ask you, do you drive a car? Let's take a drive down a two-lane highway. Coming at us is a huge Mitsubishi truck. To our right there is no guardrail, only a steep slope down a hillside. If the truck suddenly swerved into our lane, what would we do? We imagine. A plot lives in experiences we have every day, if only we would turn our imaginations loose.

We take a small child to the doctor for his scheduled vaccination. You're holding the child in your arms as the nurse approaches. The nurse takes the protective cap off the needle. You notice that a drop of red is dripping out of the needle. Red vaccine? It has to be blood. Is it contaminated blood? The nurse's expression has turned from kindly benevolence to fierce determination. "Please no," you say, trying to protect your child.

You can take any everyday occurrence and with a flick of your imagination turn it into horror. Or something else. Say your female protagonist is lying in a hospital bed, both of her legs in plaster casts. A male nurse comes in, not one she's seen before. Almost at once this handsome fellow starts taking his white uniform off. Then he begins to pull off his jeans. The woman in bed says, "Hey, what are you doing?"

If a dozen writers thought of that situation, you'd get a dozen different stories. In the first story, a female nurse holds a possibly life-threatening needle she is going to inject in a child, in the next a male nurse is a threat to the helpless patient whose legs are in a cast. Both have characteristics of melodrama. The situations are exaggerated, and the credibility of what's to happen is marred. (In Chapter Nine, I explain melodrama and its hazards at greater length.) Can your imagination lead you to more-realistic plot lines, drawn from something that may have happened to someone you know, or that you fear might happen to you?

Any incident can be taken in a number of directions. Let's suppose the first nurse has an ordinary needle, no blood at its tip. She looks at the baby in your arms, and a worry appears in her eyes. She puts the cap back on the needle and says, "One moment, I'll get the doctor." We have no idea what she's observed, only that there's something wrong with the baby. That generates tension and suspense for a different kind of story. What I'm trying to suggest is that almost every ordinary circumstance in life, from driving a car to taking a child to the doctor, can be manipulated by a released imagination to create a situation that will move the reader. Faulkner once said, "With me a story usually begins with a single idea or memory or mental picture. The writing of the story is simply a matter of working up to that moment, to explain why it happened or what caused it to follow."

Years ago someone suggested that what my novels had in common was that each had a theme that would become a subject of public discussion a couple of years later. My first novel was about divorce, a word that then could not be used on certain televison shows. My second was about a teenager rebelling against the injustice in the so-called justice system as well as an exposure of the rackets that existed in high schools countrywide. My next was about a woman of twenty-seven trying to succeed in the then-male-dominated advertising business. I am not clairvoyant, and my novels certainly don't cause the public interest in their subject matter. I suspect that when a subject seems fresh to me, it may be in the minds of many people at the time, getting ready to go public, as it were, the only difference being that as a writer I turn my thoughts into stories that see print. *A writer writes what other people only think.* What we've been doing here is converting momentary observations into characters, and our freewheeling thoughts into the beginnings of a story.

One plotting technique that's been of special value to me is the crucible, to which I devoted a chapter in *Stein on Writing*. A story's tension can be heightened enormously if the characters are caught in a place they can't leave. Think of a lifeboat, a prison, an army, a family. In the case of *The Magician*, the hero and the villain are both sixteen-year-olds caught in the same crucible, a high school. Neither boy can leave. I've used this technique in other novels, and commend it to you.

In an interview years ago, Kurt Vonnegut rattled off familiar plots:

> Somebody gets into trouble, and then gets out again; somebody loses something and gets it back; somebody is wronged and gets revenge; Cinderella; somebody hits the skids and just goes down, down, down; people fall in love with each other, and a lot of other people get in the way; a virtuous person is falsely accused of sin; a sinful person is believed to be virtuous; a person faces a challenge bravely, and succeeds or fails; a person lies, a person steals, a person kills, a person commits fornication.

When the interviewer commented that these were old-fashioned plots, Vonnegut was quick to reply.

> I guarantee you that no modern story scheme, even plotlessness, will give a reader genuine satisfaction unless one of those old-fashioned plots is smuggled in somewhere. I don't praise plots as accurate representations of life, but as ways to keep readers reading.

Vonnegut's list isn't complete, of course, but it makes the point. Others over the years have itemized "all" available plots. Some new plot ideas develop as a result of social or technological change. If you were to assign any of those "old-fashioned" plots to a hundred writers, they'd come up with a hundred different stories. As long as individual imaginations differ, you don't have to worry about someone having used the basic plot earlier.

To recap the craft points stressed in this chapter:

1. Try to state the idea or concept of your story in a sentence or two. It can be done even with some of the most complex literary classics. Eliminate everything from your description except the essential story.
2. Plot consists of the scenes that develop the story. The scene outline suggested earlier in this book is an ideal way of evolving a plot.
3. Make sure that each scene you develop in your plot moves the essential story forward. This doesn't exclude subplots or even interesting digressions, as long as the reader does not lose the forward momentum of the basic story in the process.

For additional guidance on plotting, see the last chapter, "Where Writers Get Help."

SEVEN

Our Native Language Is Not Dialogue

Dialogue is a language that is foreign to most writers of nonfiction and many newcomers to fiction. Totally different from whatever language a writer grows up using, dialogue is also a triumphant language. It can make people unknown to the author cry, laugh, and believe lies in seconds. It is succinct, but can carry a great weight of meaning. In a theater, dialogue can draw thunderous applause from people who have paid heavily for the privilege of listening to it. At its best, as in Shakespeare's best, dialogue provides us with memorable—and beautiful—guides for understanding the behavior of the human race.

The proof of dialogue's difference from and superiority to everyday speech is in every court transcript. Reading transcripts is a yawn. Enjoying reading them is an impossibility. Pity the poor law clerks who have to read these day after day. Most people could not read three hundred pages of continuous transcript even if they were paid well. The same is true for any exact transcription of words spoken, for almost all talk originates in the top of the head, from which we spin out whatever facts, lies, and suppositions come to mind.

All talk is first draft. We hem, haw, er, and wander—which has come to be perfectly acceptable as a way of communicating because we instinctively gather up any facts from the fluff. When a writer puts words on the page into the mouths of characters, those words had better not resemble recorded talk. Dialogue has to make us interested, curious, tense, or laugh. At its best, it has a liveliness that makes the words seem to jump from the page straight into our bloodstream, like adrenaline. Readers *enjoy* dialogue. I've never heard anyone say they enjoyed a transcript of recorded speech. If you wander around a crowded mall these days, much of what you might overhear is idiot talk. People won't buy a novel to hear idiot talk. They get that free from relatives, friends, and strangers. Readers want something special, dialogue that excites. In life, the intention of the speaker is to answer questions that are asked. Dialogue often postpones the answer to create suspense. We compliment a speaker by acknowledging that he is direct. Dialogue, to the contrary, is indirect. The most important key to understanding this new language is that dialogue involves *oblique* responses as often as possible. Non sequiturs, words that don't follow from what came before, are bothersome in talk, but add flavor in dialogue. In dialogue, logic goes out the window, followed by grammar. Dialogue is a highly crafted language with a grammar of its own. Thankfully, the techniques of dialogue can be learned by writers eager to please their readers.

I'm lucky in having started out as a playwright working within the rigors of that trade, where the only words of the writer heard by his audience are dialogue. It had better be good. When I write novels, I am tempted to use dialogue often. The minute characters talk, the reader sees them. And we know readers much prefer seeing what's happening rather than hearing about it through narration. Not to be lightly dismissed are those white spaces on the page created by exchanges of dialogue. They make the reader feel the story is moving fast.

Do you know what the most frequently used word in real speech is? It is "Uh." "Uh" is totally useless to the writer. It's what people say before, after, and in the middle of a sentence to borrow time to think of what they want to say. "Uhs" and "ers" are to be avoided in dialogue. Dialogue is a language in which every word counts. The cry in the writer's ear is *Move the story*.

Most exchanges in dialogue should be brief. A speech should be not more than three sentences. If a speech has to run longer, break it up with interruptions from other speakers or by an action or a thought. The exceptions are few. In the first of my plays, Napoleon has a long speech in which he converts a group of soldiers from hostility to loyalty. In a novel, a lawyer's recap in the courtroom can be longer as it marshals words for their cumulative impact.

For the reader, dialogue is meant to be experienced, not studied. Some of the dialogue I see in manuscript is involuted, complex, difficult to digest in a quick reading. Halting over a line of dialogue can interrupt the reader's experience. It is important to understand that the reader perceives thoughts serially, one at a time, which is why dialogue that builds is so effective when sentences are flung one after another, and each adds to the force of the whole. Leslie Fiedler, one of the important literary critics of our time, whose many books I edited, has an intricate style that might be described as parenthetical. That is, he has thoughts within thoughts. That characteristic doesn't work in dialogue because thoughts within thoughts put the reader into a deciphering rather than an experiencing mode. Dialogue that is short, snappy, punchy, engages other characters as well as the reader.

Life is full of routine exchanges. "How are you?" "I am fine." "How's the family?" All those usual questions on greeting someone are boring as dialogue, which thrives on surprise and indirection. Witness:

She: Hello there! How are you?
He: On my way to jail.
She: Good God, what are you planning to do?
He: It's done.

This exchange raises more questions than it answers, which is good. The main purpose of dialogue is to reveal character and to move a story along. The example above obviously gets a story going.

Let's look at simple examples of dialogue that reveals character.

She: I see you're feeling better.
He: Since when can you see what I feel?
She: I thought this was going to be a peaceful discussion.
He: That was yesterday.

We've only had two lines each, but it is safe to say that the woman is temperate and wants a harmonious relationship, the man is intemperate, difficult, and quick to anger.

Dialogue is at its best when it is confrontational and adversarial. It can be either or both. Talk is an action. And when talk is tough and combative, it can be much more exciting than physical action. In that excitement, the writer is liable to make a mistake. He will take sides with one of the characters.

Does the writer take sides?

Indeed he does, he takes *both sides* and gives each its due. And here's a hint. If in a verbal duel you find yourself wedded to the beliefs of one of the characters, try your damndest to make the other character win the argument. You won't succeed. But do try to subvert your prejudices. It will make your exchanges far more interesting.

Character most reveals itself in dialogue under stress. Stressed characters will blurt things out that they never meant to say. They can also be defensive, as in the following example:

> "I am not nervous, I just can't stand being called for jury duty. I walk into the courthouse, I think I'm the one that's on trial. For what? I've never even gone through a yellow light."

Characters also reveal themselves when they are angry. Example:

> "My missus and me been in this jammed waiting room for two solid hours. Not one person has been ushered in. What's the doctor doing? How many patients does a doctor need in his waiting room to satisfy his ego? Our kid, he was supposed to be picked up fifteen minutes ago. I can't phone the sidewalk outside the school, I've got to get out of here and leave the missus to hear the bad news of her tests all alone. Jesus, why can't these stethescope generals keep appointments like other people?"

The aim of dialogue is to create an emotional effect in the reader. One of the things a writer has to learn by conscious application is to discard the coherence and logic that he aimed for in his nonfiction writings in the past. Dialogue sounds artificial when it is coherent and logical. You want thoughts that are loose, words that tumble out.

In life, we try to avoid shouting. It shows that we are out of control. And we don't like it when other people shout at us. Someone else's anger makes us queasy, uncomfortable, eager to get away. Readers love to hear shouting if the tone is carried by the words rather than by the author telling the reader that a character is shouting.

Shouting can be dramatic if anger is responded to with anger, but perhaps even more dramatic if the anger is opposed by an attempt to pacify or to resolve, especially if the anger continues. Listen to the supervisor in the following exchange:

> "Don't you knock before you come in?"
> "I'm sorry, I—"
> "Can it. I've heard all the excuses—you blew your last chance, that's it."
> "It wasn't my fault. Judy can tell you—"
> "I don't want you involving Judy, George, Carey, anybody. It was you who didn't. Look, I've had enough—just pack, get your things, and get out of here."

I chose this exchange because without the context you don't know who did what, but we get a sense of the supervisor's anger not only in what he says, but also in the looseness of his disjointed comments. What comes across is the strength of his emotion, and to the extent that what he says seems unfair to the other person, the emotion transfers to the reader.

What can you say about the student in the following exchange?

Teacher: Tell me about yourself.
Student: I'm just a boy.
Teacher: All the boys here are boys. What's different about you?
Student: Nothing, I have a mother and a sister and I do my homework every day.
Teacher: You left out your father.

Student: It's not my fault. He left himself out.
Teacher: Did you forget to mention him?
Student: He took off. He doesn't even phone.
Teacher: Do you know where he is? Can you get in touch?
Student: He isn't anywhere. He could be dead and I wouldn't know!

The boy is trying not to reveal to his teacher or classmates the secret that makes him different. When he is forced to reveal it, the reader is immediately sympathetic. A character who reveals *not enough* reveals much.

To sum up, a character reveals himself most readily when under stress, blurting things out, saying things in anger that are normally suppressed, saying not enough, saying too much.

Before you begin writing any new dialogue, know the purpose of the exchange. How will you orchestrate it to make it adversarial? If a conflict between the characters speaking already exists, does the exchange exacerbate that conflict or at least increase the tension between the characters? After completing an exchange, or when revising the scene it's in, check to see if the lines spoken by each character are consistent with that character's background. Weed out any unnecessary words. Loosen stiff sentences. Substitute colloquial expressions for formal expressions. And perhaps most important, check to see what's going on between the lines. What counts in dialogue is not what is said but what is meant.

I find it useful to think of dialogue as analogous to the action in America's national sport of baseball, which has taken hold in Japan, Mexico, Cuba, and Russia.

The basics needed for this demonstration are simple enough.

The pitcher on one team throws the ball toward a strike zone over home plate next to the batter. His aim is to deliver strikes three times to strike out the batter. He can do this by brushing the corners of the invisible box of the strike zone. The pitcher can cause the batter to hit the ball high so that it will be caught before it hits the ground, or along the ground, enabling the hit ball to be scooped up and thrown to first base, arriving there before the batter does.

To accomplish this, the pitcher uses a number of different kinds of pitches, each of which has an equivalent in dialogue. A good pitcher surprises the batter. A good exchange in dialogue surprises the reader.

Let's take our imaginations to a baseball game in which there is no batter, therefore no adversary. The onlookers would quickly get bored watching the pitcher doing his fancy stuff and the catcher returning the ball lackadaisically.

Now let's imagine a different scenario. The catcher doesn't like the first pitch that comes to him. He throws the ball back just as hard as it came to him. The pitcher is surprised. He decides to make the next pitch even harder. The catcher almost drops the ball. What's the pitcher trying to do? Has he forgotten that the catcher is on the same team? The catcher throws the ball back even harder at the pitcher's ungloved hand. The ball stings the pitcher's hand. Furious, he throws a wild pitch. The catcher misses it, and loses his balance. What's going on here?

What's going on is that the pitcher and the catcher have become adversaries, and their rivalry becomes interesting to watch. That's exactly what enhances exchanges in dialogue.

In an actual baseball game the pitcher attempts to surprise the batter by making the ball behave differently from how the batter expects it to behave. To help us understand the varieties of dialogue that carry an element of surprise and are different from conventional speech, let's examine some comparisons that will help get the hang of this new language.

A curveball doesn't look as if it's going to cross the strike zone until the very last split second. Or it curves out of the strike zone, causing the batter to miss the ball. Here's an Elmore Leonard character propositioning a woman with a curveball:

"Let's get a drink and talk for a few days."

The sentence starts with a commonplace invitation ("Let's get a drink") and ends with a proposition. The reader enjoys the surprise. If I were to send you to a single contemporary writer to examine his dialogue, it would be to Elmore Leonard. His characters are oddball stereotypes of rough hombres who have minimal complexity. They are not the characters of mainstream fiction that we remember with affection. The stories they are involved in seem fabricated, even to people who rush to read each new bestseller from Elmore Leonard's pen. I am convinced that much of the popularity of Elmore Leonard's books rests in the entertaining effectiveness of his dialogue. It is not surprising that at last count seventeen of Elmore Leonard's novels have been bought for the movies, where dialogue is what survives in the translation from paper to screen. If you browse through some of his novels, you'll see that he uses far more dialogue than most writers.

Now let's take our baseball analogy further. A fastball rockets toward the strike zone over home plate at high speeds of nearly one hundred miles an hour. Here's the equivalent in dialogue:

"You should have seen Ziggie—bursts in, stuffs a suitcase, zips out the door, gets behind the wheel, and gone."

A sinker is a pitch that seems to be heading into the strike zone but drops below it at the last moment, causing the batter to miss. Here's an example of an outstanding sinker by Ross MacDonald:

> "Thalassa, the sea, the Homeric sea. We could build another Athens. I used to think we could do it in San Francisco, build a new city of man on the great hills. A city measured with forgiveness. Oh, well."

A sinker can be especially useful in comedy dialogue.

> "Are you going to let go of me or shall I scream and let the neighbors see you in your undershirt?"

A knuckleball has an irregular flight that makes it hard to hit. Neither pitcher, catcher, batter, nor anyone else knows what its flight path will be. It has its equivalent in dialogue.

Man: This is my key.
Friend: Can you find your car?
Man: It's in the damn lot, isn't it. That's where I left it. It's got to be where I left it, right?
Friend: You'd better let me drive.

In life, out-of-control conversation is annoying. In books, readers love non sequiturs and dialogue that jumps around illogically and yet seems to follow.

The point to remember about all of these examples is that dialogue is not an exchange of information but a kind of game in which the opponents try to gain an advantage over each other.

Consider some examples from an indoor sport. Table tennis or

Ping-Pong is played by opponents with paddles across a table with a net in the middle. An uninteresting exchange in Ping-Pong has the opponents hitting the ball back and forth across the middle of the net, pip, pop, pip, pop, pip, pop, like a metronome. To break the monotony and win, an opponent may try to put a spin on the ball so that when it bounces, it will go in an unexpected direction or suddenly lose its momentum. A player can also smash the ball so that it bounces high off the table, making it impossible for the opponent to return. The oblique return, you may have guessed by now, is the return of the ball somewhere else than where it is expected. Let's look at some examples in dialogue for the spin, the smash, and the oblique return.

The spin is a form of dialogue in which the speaker seems to change his direction within one speech, much like the sinker in the baseball analogy:

He: Come on, let's go.
She: I'm not coming. Not now, anyway. Maybe later.

The smash is a normal exchange that suddenly takes on ferocity:

She: It's marvelous outside. The leaves are changing color.
He: I'm reading the paper.
She: Read the paper later, John, the leaves may not wait till tomorrow.
He: I have a reservation.
She: About going out?
He: A reservation on a plane.
She: What plane?
He: Out of O'Hare. I've got to get away from here.
She: I thought you loved this house.
He: It's not the house, it's you.

The best dialogue is oblique. It characterizes instantly and involves the reader's emotions in the story.

Think of dialogue exchanges as confrontations or interrogations. Let's look at a confrontation first. In the following exchange, the head of a major advertising agency, Amory, receives a call from Shipman, the producer of a television interview show who invited Amory to appear as a guest and is calling back for a decision. The conversation is done from Amory's point of view. His thoughts can therefore be used to break up the dialogue. I've chosen this example to show how a longish thought of the viewpoint character can add rather than subtract tension from a confrontational exchange.

> "Good morning to you, Mr. Shipman. Question. Anyone ever turn a Ketchum interview down?"
>
> "Arafat didn't. George Bush and Boris Yeltsin didn't. Are you about to?"
>
> "I bet they all regretted it."
>
> Shipman's laugh had a smoker's rasp. "The president's committed for the sixteenth."
>
> Amory said, "He's got guts, but he'll regret it. Why the hell is Ketchum doing me? J. Walter Thompson is still number one."
>
> "Not for long if you keep it up. Off the pot, Mr. Amory. Every advertiser with a pocketbook has someone watching Jenny's show. The interview gets you exposure you couldn't pay for."
>
> That interview might draw a new client or two, as other interviews had. People in the street would recognize his face without quite remembering where they saw it. They'd stop

him, believing he was someone they knew whose name they'd forgotten. What does notoriety get you, a better table in a restaurant you'd rather not eat in?

Amory remembered being taken to a Broadway opening as a boy. Exiting through the crowd in single file between velvet ropes, his mother in front of him pointed out Luise Rainer, unrecognized among the celebrities. Suddenly, the elderly actress pulled her hat down over her face, causing the crowd to shriek, "Who is she? Who is she?" Apparently none of them recognized the two-time Oscar winner.

Fame fizzles like water in an empty skillet.

"Well Mr. Amory," Jack Shipman said, "I'm waiting for your answer."

Amory was thinking about the way Jenny Ketchum's lips opened just before she said "Good evening" to her public.

Shipman said, "Jenny's doing Kissinger next. If you have reservations, I'll move Kissinger up to your time slot. You going forward or backing out? Which?"

In this confrontation, one character, Shipman, is pressing for an answer—and not getting it. The person who is supposed to be responding has a different script. He is thinking of the downside. That creates the tension in the exchange.

Now let's examine dialogue in an interrogation scene. Long thoughts would be inappropriate, but you need "beats" in the dialogue, a term writers use for small actions that help keep a scene visual and that can add tension to an exchange. Here a detective is interrogating the television interviewer. Notice the three methods that are used in this scene to create adversarial tension. First, impatience. Second, misunderstandings. Third, the characters have different intentions, and the intentions clash.

He held out a hand, looked Jenny up and down, then led the way. Over his shoulder he said, "I'm Detective Laren." He gestured, "Take a seat, Miss Ketchum. I've seen your show almost regular. Coffee?"

Jenny shook her head. "My son Zeke was eight years old today. We were at the movies—"

"I've got an all points out, black pick-up make unknown, eight-year-old boy, unidentified man. Miss Ketchum . . ."

Detective Laren handed her a Kleenex box. She drew two tissues, blew her nose in one and used the other to wipe her hair, which was stupid because pieces of Kleenex stuck like wet snow.

"You got a picture of your boy on you?"

She foraged in her purse, pushing the familiar objects aside, there it was, the celluloid thing she kept Zeke's pictures in. She flipped to the most recent shot of Zeke holding onto the thick vine choking the big maple, making like Tarzan. She had trouble slipping the snapshot out of the celluloid. Her fingers were not obeying her. She handed the whole thing over to the detective, with the Tarzan picture showing. "It was taken more than a year ago."

"That's good."

"What's good?"

"He's got a dimple. What's this?"

"He fell against the corner of a glass coffee table when he was little. It's a small scar."

"How tall is he?"

Jenny told him.

"Weight?"

"He's skinny."

"That's not a weight, is it?"

"I think the nurse at the pediatrician's said sixty-eight. Does that matter? You going to ask every kid you see with an adult if he weighs sixty-eight pounds?"

Laren looked at her. "This is what we do. Height, weight, clothing. What was he wearing? Please don't tell me clothes. I need type, colors, specifics."

Detective Laren wrote down what Jenny told him. Then he looked at her the way she looked at one of her interviewees when she was about to launch a zinger. "Is there a Mr. Ketchum."

"My father in South Dakota."

Laren looked up from the form. "What I'm asking is about the father of the missing child."

"The father's name is Daniel Goodridge."

"You're not Mrs. Goodridge?"

"I use the name that's on my birth certificate." Simmer down, the man needs his form filled out.

"Did your husband accompany you to the movies?"

"No."

"He stayed home? You want to call him?"

"We're separated."

"Divorced?"

"Not yet." Laren had an unasked question on his face. "I said not yet!"

"When you ask questions, Miss Ketchum, do people shout at you? I'd sure appreciate it if you'd keep your voice down. The other officers here are trying to help people like I'm trying to help you find your boy."

"I'm sorry. I didn't mean to raise my voice." Jenny noticed the tremor in her left hand. She let it touch the desk to still it, but it continued its involuntary agitation as if it had a life of its own. Whenever she'd seen a quiver in someone's face or limbs, she thought of it as a weakness. She noticed her right hand was also trembling. She hid both hands in her lap.

"I realize you're under a strain," Detective Laren said. "Nine out of ten kids what's missing are taken by the other spouse. You think your husband . . ."

Jenny got herself to her feet, still clasping her hands. A detective at a nearby desk looked up from his work. She said, "The man who took Zeke didn't look anything like my husband."

"We'd like to talk to your husband. We'd like him to come in. Please sit down. You can use this phone."

Jenny scavenged through her purse for her address book. Where was it? Why was she looking, she knew Dan's number by heart.

"Dial nine first," Detective Laren said.

The use of *impatience* increases tension. The detective has his form to fill out. The mother of the child is answering the questions, but not the way the detective wants the answers. He gets impatient, the tension rises.

Adding *misunderstandings* is a useful technique. Detective Laren asks for the boy's weight. The mother replies that he's skinny. Laren can't write "skinny" down on his form, he needs a weight. Temper flares, tension increases.

A third and more fundamental means of providing tension consists of giving each speaker a different underlying attitude. This is based on a technique developed in the Playwrights Group of the Actors Studio. Writers are troublemakers. The detective and the woman have different scripts. She is an experienced celebrity television interviewer, used to asking questions, not answering them. The detective knows who she is, and his attitude is that right now she's not a celebrity television interviewer but a mother supplying detail needed for his investigation. Like any bureaucrat, he wants her to conform to what he expects her conduct to be. With these differing scripts, the interrogation throws sparks. That's what readers like.

Notice that when the woman hands the picture collection over to the detective, he says, "That's good," and she hasn't a clue to what's good. What the detective notices right away, because it's his job to notice, is that the boy has a dimple, which is the kind of identifying mark that he is looking for. When he asks the boy's weight, he gets an unsatisfactory answer, unsatisfactory to Detective Laren maybe, but satisfactory to the reader.

When Laren asks, "Is there a Mr. Ketchum?" the likelihood is that the woman knows what he wants, but she gives him an answer that he can only view as smart-alecky. This establishes a difference in their social background. He comes from a world in which a wife takes the husband's name. The woman, younger and more sophisticated, like many professional women uses her maiden name. Those background differences are at the heart of fiction. Whenever you are doing a dialogue exchange, think of the background of the characters, where they differ most, and how such differences can be used to heat up their dialogue.

You now have three techniques to use in making dialogue interesting: impatience, misunderstandings, and differing underlying attitudes. Dialogue is not a recording of speech, it is an invented language. As a refresher, let's now remind ourselves of some basic guidelines for dialogue:

1. What counts in dialogue is not what is said but what is meant.
2. Whenever possible, dialogue should be adversarial. Think of dialogue as confrontations or interrogations. Remember, combat can be subtle.

3. The best dialogue contains responses that are indirect, oblique.
4. Dialogue is illogical. Non sequiturs are fine. So are incomplete sentences, and occasional faulty grammar suited to the character.
5. Dialogue, compared to actual speech, is terse. If a speech runs over three sentences, you may be speechifying. In accusatory confrontations, however, longer speeches can increase tension if the accusations build.
6. Tension can be increased by the use of misunderstandings, impatience, and especially by giving the characters in a scene different scripts.
7. Characters reveal themselves best in dialogue when they lose their cool and start blurting things out.
8. Think of the analogies with baseball and Ping-Pong as a way of understanding how dialogue differs from ordinary exchanges. In life, adversarial or heated exchanges tend to be repetitive; in dialogue, such exchanges build. In life, adversarial exchanges vent the speakers' emotions; in dialogue, such exchanges are designed to move a story forward.
9. Avoid dialect. It makes readers see words on the page and interrupts their experience.
10. In dialogue every word counts. Be ruthless in eliminating excess verbiage. All talk is first draft. Dialogue is not talk.

EIGHT

Getting Intimate with the Reader: Advanced Point of View

This is a chapter about opportunities. Frequently missed opportunities.

Point of view is possibly the most mismanaged aspect of the writer's craft. It is also one of the most poorly taught subjects. I have eavesdropped on sessions where the instructor explaining point of view seemed to be as bewildered as her students.

Point of view, or POV, is simply the perspective from which a scene is written, which character's eyes and mind are witnessing the events. Here is a skeleton of the basic possibilities:

First-person point of view: *I saw this, I did that.* This is the most intimate, immediately involving mode. The "I" character speaks to the reader directly. This POV has become increasingly common in literary and mainstream fiction. The writer becomes an impersonator. His voice, mind, and background are those of the character he is impersonating. This chapter covers the sequential impersonation of different characters in the same story.

Second-person point of view: *You saw this, you did that.* Forget second person. It is rarely used in fiction, for good reason. It talks to the reader as if the reader were a character in the story. It comes across as artificial. It can make the reader aware of the storytelling rather than involving the reader in the experience of the story.

Third-person point of view: *He saw this, he did that.* Third-person POV is the most common in popular fiction. It is easier to do than first person. The discipline involved is in keeping the point of view to one character for as long as possible within a scene. The more shifting around the author does, the more the writing will seem out of control.

Omniscient point of view: The perspective is anybody's. This is probably the easiest point of view for the beginning writer—and the most dangerous. It is like the undisciplined free verse of beginners that cries out for rhythm and structure. The writer is a god. He can see everything everywhere. Because the writer flits about from character to character, often thoughtlessly, the result can be more like alphabet soup than a controlled experience for the reader. Most inexpert fiction that has come my way is maimed by *uncontrolled* third-person or omniscient point of view.

There are variations and subcategories of these points of view that bewilder the newcomer and entangle the experienced writer. Simplify your thinking. First person, third person, omniscient if you have to.

Handling point of view is like skating on ice. When it goes well, it's an intricate dance, beautifully performed. When the point of view shifts without the writer being aware of it, the thin ice cracks. The reader doesn't know anything about point of view. He knows only that the dance seems momentarily out of control. If the slippage continues, the reader may put the book down and pick up another book. I can't recall a manuscript by a professional writer that didn't have a couple of glitches in the handling of point of view. Sometimes dozens. They need to be caught in revision. The novelist's authority depends on it.

Before we can seize the opportunities that abound in advanced handling of point of view, some historical perspective. In centuries before the twentieth, the story was often told by a narrator. Some of the great novels of the early twentieth century—I think of *The Good Soldier* by Ford Madox Ford and *The Great Gatsby* by Scott Fitzgerald—are told by a narrator who is a character in the story. After the explosion of film and TV in the twentieth century, readers insisted on seeing a story rather than hearing about it. The primary sense—sight—became dominant in fiction. The writer now knows he must show the story, not tell it, which is why I have emphasized the plotting and organizing of stories in visible scenes. We know that scenes are most effective when the point of view is from the character most affected by what happens in the scene. Perhaps this is why I favor first person, although not for everyone, and certainly not for the writer who has difficulty impersonating his characters. Impersonation is like getting a new skin, a new attitude, a new voice. To be a different person for a while is an ideal opportunity for the creative writer.

In 1998 Knopf published a remarkable first novel that one reviewer called "a startling act of literary impersonation." *Memoirs of a Geisha* is the story of a Japanese geisha from the age of nine, told in the first person by a white American male named Arthur Golden, born in Chattanooga, Tennessee, and educated at Harvard, Columbia, and Boston universities. Called "astonishing" and "breathtaking" by reviewers, and propelled by the word of mouth of readers, *Memoirs of a Geisha* was on the national bestseller lists for more than a year. Here's how it begins.

Suppose that you and I were sitting in a quiet room overlooking a garden, chatting and sipping at our cups of green tea while we talked about something that had happened a long while ago, and I said to you, "That afternoon when I met so-and-so . . . was the very best afternoon of my life, and also the very worst afternoon." I expect you might put down your teacup and say, "Well, now which was it? Was it the best or the worst? Because it can't possibly have been both!" Ordinarily I'd have to laugh at myself and agree with you. But the truth is that the afternoon when I met Mr. Tanaka Ichiro really was the best and the worst of my life. He seemed so fascinating to me, even the fish smell on his hands was a kind of perfume. If I had never known him, I'm sure I would not have become a geisha.

I wasn't born and raised to be a Kyoto geisha. I wasn't even born in Kyoto. I'm a fisherman's daughter from a little town called Yoroido on the Sea of Japan. In all my life I've never told more than a handful of people anything at all about Yoroido, or about the house in which I grew up, or about my mother and father, or my older sister—and certainly not about how I became a geisha, or what it was like to be one. Most people would much rather carry on with their fantasies that my mother and grandmother were geisha, and that I began my training in dance when I was weaned from the breast, and so on. As a matter of fact, one day many years ago I was pouring a cup of sake for a man who happened to mention that he had been in Yoroido only the previous week. Well, I felt as a bird must feel when it has flown across the ocean and comes upon a creature that knows its nest. I was so shocked I couldn't stop myself from saying:

"Yoroido! Why, that's where I grew up!"

This poor man! His face went through the most remarkable series of changes. He tried his best to smile, though it didn't come out well because he couldn't get the look of shock off his face.

"Yoroido?" he said. "You can't mean it."

I long ago developed a very practiced smile, which I call my "Noh smile" because it resembles a Noh mask whose features are frozen. Its advantage is that men can interpret it however they want; you can imagine how often I've relied on it. I decided I'd better use it just then, and of course it worked. He let out all his breath and tossed down the cup of sake I'd poured for him before giving an enormous laugh I'm sure was prompted more by relief than anything else.

"The very idea!" he said, with another big laugh. "You, growing up in a dump like Yoroido. That's like making tea in a bucket!" And when he'd laughed again, he said to me, "That's why you're so much fun, Sayuri-san. Sometimes you almost make me believe your little jokes are real."

I don't much like thinking of myself as a cup of tea made in a bucket, but I suppose in a way it must be true. After all, I did grow up in Yoroido, and no one would suggest it's a glamorous spot. Hardly anyone ever visits it. As for the people who live there, they never have occasion to leave. You're probably wondering how I came to leave it myself. That's where my story begins.

For the novelist, *Memoirs of a Geisha* is a doubly rewarding experience, worth studying to see how it is possible to get into the head of a character who is foreign in every sense but human. The author is male, the geisha female, the author is American, the geisha is Japanese, the societies have different customs, values, possibilities. Now hear this: *Great actors do this all the time.* Think of

Laurence Olivier as Henry V and then think of him as Archie in *The Comedian.* The difference is this: The actors impersonate roles written by writers. Our work comes first.

When the writer impersonates a character in the first-person point of view, it is through that character's eyes that everything is seen. It is what that character hears, smells, touches, and tastes that the reader senses. It is that character's brain that thinks about what he sees, and that gives depth to the reader's experience. The writer is inside the head of the character, speaking with that character's voice, knowledge, and background. I don't know a form of fiction writing that is more fun.

One used to run into a frequent objection to the first-person point of view because, ostensibly, you couldn't show scenes at which the character was not present. Nonsense. Someone was there, and that someone and your first-person character can have an adversarial exchange about what that someone reports. Some writers shy away from the first-person point of view because they foresee difficulty in conveying what the speaker looks like. It's easy enough to have another character tell your first-person character what he looks like.

> Morris said, "Did you lose your comb? Your face looks like parchment. Your nose is larger than when I last saw you poking it into other people's business."
>
> I said, "I've had a hard day, Morris. I'll take tomorrow off and by evening I'll look like Cary Grant."

It's an old dodge to have characters seeing themselves in a mirror. I shamefully resorted to that in *The Best Revenge.*

A few writers I've talked to avoid first person because they fear monotony. Is Huckleberry Finn monotonous? Is Holden Caulfield? Their voices are distinctive. What is even more exciting for the experienced fiction writer is creating several distinctive impersonations, using multiple first-person points of view in the same story.

Many people became aware of the advantages of this technique when two short stories by Ryunosuke Akutagawa were made into the remarkable film *Rashomon* by the great Akira Kurosawa. Against its twelfth-century background, four characters, a woman, her husband, a bandit who rapes the wife in front of her husband, and a woodcutter who sees it all, relate serially what happened in the same incident. The versions don't jibe, they disagree with each other, adding conflict and tension. This form opens up the imaginative possibilities in fiction. The writer-impersonator can choose characters with different sexes, ages, and especially from different social and cultural backgrounds, providing the clash of background and upbringing among the characters that is the essence of fiction. The writer provides different scripts to each character, enhancing, as in *Rashomon*, the conflict, tension, and interest.

First person strengthens credibility. We know the character's thoughts, even when they differ from what he says or does. When a character is deceiving another character, the reader knows what he's up to. Wonderful!

Though my novels have been written in both the first and third person, I have an inclination toward the first person because it so quickly establishes an intimacy with the reader. I enjoy impersonating both sexes, every age, foreigners as well as Americans, the educated and the street-smart, characters with snobbish origins, and those who are not sure who their own parents are. Readers familiar with my work know that I believe differences in social background are the key to drama and fiction, and when these differences clash, I welcome the chance to impersonate both sides in the first person. Bernard Shaw, let us remember, was the true father of both Liza Doolittle and Henry Higgins.

I have dealt with these opportunities in two ways. In *The Magician*, an early novel of mine written ostensibly in the third person, I sneak in comments (labeled as such), interruptions by other characters, each of whom speaks in the first person. It is a composite form. While the book received welcome attention from book critics, not a single review referred to the mixture of third and first person, though the intrusions were direct. The controlled mix of points of view remained invisible to the reader. I couldn't be pleased more.

The book begins with a third-person perspective. The protagonist, as you may know by now, is a sixteen-year-old named Ed Japhet. The third-person section that begins the book ends with the following exchange by the protagonist's parents:

> "I have a feeling," Mrs. Japhet said to her husband one night as they decided to go up to bed, "that Ed is headed for a fascinating career."
>
> Mr. Japhet, after a moment's reflection, said, "I have a feeling we have provided him with the capability of getting into trouble."
>
> He proved right, of course.

That is followed by an interjection by Mr. Japhet, as if he were hearing the story along with the reader. Note that within parentheses I identify him by name, and baldly give his age and occupation. Nobody, not my editor, publisher, or any reviewer or reader ever objected to this directness.

Comment by His Father

(Terence Japhet, age 46, teacher)

I've been teaching at Ossining High for fourteen years. It's awkward having your son a student in the same school. The rule is he can't be in my class. We sometimes pass each other in the halls in the morning, and I say, "Hello, Ed," even though I may have seen him over breakfast, and he usually waves, but he doesn't say, "Hi, Dad," even though the friends he's with know who I am, of course.

When this thing happened at the prom, I mean the show itself, I wasn't there and heard about it secondhand, from teachers, students, Ed himself; and not all the versions jibe. People always ask me how he does his tricks. I don't have anything to do with his magic; he just started it as a kind of hobby when he was about twelve, bought a few mail-order tricks, built some equipment in my downstairs workshop, then started attending these magicians' meetings in New York and getting better at it. The hobby seems to have had a constructive effect. A central interest is what I mean, something he fusses with every day, especially weekends.

But I can't believe that the danger he found himself in was an accident. In a world that affects egalitarianism, the cardinal sin is to make yourself conspicuous.

Comment by His Girl Friend

(Lila Hurst, age 16, student)

People think a girl notices first how a fellow looks. Well, Ed looks, you know, tall, blondish hair and all that, his face is okay even if his right ear sticks out a little, but lots of fellows have okay looks. I guess what I first liked about Ed was his manner. Most boys his age are elbows and knees, they don't stand up right, but Ed stands and walks like he was somebody great, and I don't mean pompous-ass, though I know inside he's not that secure. Except when he's doing his magic tricks.

We started dating, nothing special. We liked each other's company more than we liked hanging around with the others. The grown-ups think we go off and bang all the time because we're alone. Of course, everything has changed since the prom. I wish it had never happened.

Encouraged by the reception of my experiment in *The Magician*, I adventured further in a novel entitled *Other People*, in which each of the ten main characters speaks in the first person. As a test of impersonation, I used first person for both sexes and the markedly different social classes involved in the story. The novel starts with the first-person voice of an educated and well-bred—perhaps a bit stuffy—person.

When I telephoned Thomassy that morning in March of 1974 and asked him to lunch, I counseled myself to muster a casual voice. As I waited for him to get on the line, I thought *the protections are gone.* I had reluctantly perceived that civil and well-educated people now accepted gratuitous violence against strangers as ordinary. Therefore I had to conclude that George Thomassy had chosen an appropriate profession in criminal law and I had not.

The vocabulary—phrases like "I counseled myself" and words like "muster," "gratuitous," "appropriate"—suggests the kind of person he is. He persuades the criminal lawyer, Thomassy, to have lunch with him. Thomassy, it will soon turn out, is the principal adult male character of this story, and so Widmer's further thoughts before they meet are about Thomassy. I am using Widmer to set up a much more important character, the lawyer who can make the justice system bend to the will of Francine Widmer.

When I report to you that Thomassy is regarded by other lawyers like myself as the best criminal lawyer in Westchester County, what is it I mean by "the best"? When a man runs a mile faster than any living human has heretofore, he has achieved an absolute, but how few of life's activities—art, pleasure, the law—can be so precisely determined! I remember William York Tindall used to say that his idea of perfection was to be able to put his legs up after a fine meal and listen to Mozart while smoking a Romeo and Julieta cigar. I knew exactly what he meant, though Mozart was by no means my favorite composer, and since the cigar makers fled Havana, Romeo and Julietas are not the smoke we once prized. If I had to be restricted to seeing one painting for the rest of my life, even if it was a Rouault or a Rembrandt, I should soon weary of it, but I can think of a small collection, perhaps a dozen or so, that might keep my eyes content. However, if you have been involved in a crime, and you need to deal with the law, you'll find that very few private individuals can hire a battery of attorneys; you usually pick one, and if the matter is important, you narrow your choice to the best. Hence Thomassy.

At Yale, even before I entered the Law School, it was made clear to me that all of the lawyers who inhabited the social echelon I came from without exception practiced civil law. Criminal lawyers, even the best, had a touch of taint. Their affairs caused them to associate not with the kind of people they would invite to their homes, but with labor racketeers, embezzlers, Sicilians, and worse. Moreover, criminal law was comparatively unremunerative except for those few lawyers who were primarily actors or outlaws.

I was not about to lose the advantage I created in *The Magician* with my interruptive comments by other characters. Within a few pages of the beginning, Widmer's first-person chapter is interrupted by George Thomassy's father:

Comment by Haig Thomassian

I talk to you the truth. I don't want to call the boy George. My wife Marya, may she rest in peace, herself named after the mother of Jesus, we are in this new country only four years, she gives birth to a son, and calls him George, an American name used by everybody, especially Greeks. He is son of successful horse dealer who owes money to nobody. He should have been christened Haig after me, or Armen after his grandfather. For me, George sounds like a foreigner.

The contrast between the immigrant Haig and the old-line WASP Widmer begins to establish the differences among the characters in the novel. Haig Thomassian's comment ends:

I tell him now is the time to move back, we have plenty crime in Oswego, good business for lawyers. He refuses me. I tell you, in his soul my son is a Turk.

Sure, on my birthdays the telephone rings, his secretary says "George Thomassy calling," and I yell at her, "Thomassian, Thomassian!" Then I hear George's voice. I feel he wants to talk, ask questions about what I do, how I feel, but I give him the least words, "yes" or "no," until he gives up. Even if he becomes the biggest lawyer in the whole United States, to me, as an Armenian, he is nothing.

The point-of-view character of this first chapter is still Archibald Widmer. It is from his POV that the reader travels to the first meeting with Thomassy. By that time the reader knows a lot about Thomassy from both Widmer and Thomassy's father. The reader knows something about Widmer from hearing Widmer talk, but as soon as the lunch meeting is over, we have another character commenting. Widmer's wife has a lot to say about her husband.

Comment by Priscilla Graves Widmer, Smith College, '40

His full nomenclature was Archibald Edward Widmer III. No one was about to call him Archie or Eddie, and Edward sounded like the Duke of Windsor so everyone in our crowd called him Ned.

What was the chemistry? He looked good in white suits. He was clean. His forearms were muscular. He blew into my ear on our first date. From the start, I trusted him to look out for my interests. He made me feel safe. Men weren't adversaries in those days. We didn't put excessive weight on orgasmic response or subject our feelings to psychoanalysis. We aimed for wedlock.

My friends thought Ned prissy. Edith's Brock concealed something behind his facade of shyness I didn't want to get in bed with. And Alison's Peter—what ambisexual lusts were camouflaged by his toothsome flash of condescension at every man, woman, and pet that came into view. My Ned was not prissy once our bedroom door was shut.

This is just a small portion of Priscilla Widmer's comment. We are a few pages into the novel, and we know a good deal about four characters: Archibald Widmer, his wife, George Thomassy, his father. This is immediately followed by a comment from the daughter, Francine Widmer. By the end of chapter one, the reader has met the principal characters, knows a lot about their backgrounds without any flashbacks, and the story has been unrolling since the first two pages in which the reader learns that Archibald Widmer's daughter has been raped, and that she is determined to force the rapist into court against a justice system that would just as soon avoid such prosecutions.

It's difficult in just a few pages here to convey the texture of the story as well as the technique of multiple first-person points of view, and the interruptions that heighten the tension. I don't want to urge this kind of advanced technique on anyone who isn't ready for it, but I do want to suggest a few additional advantages of the technique that may be helpful.

Before I wrote *Other People*, besides *Rashomon* I'd seen only a couple of television movies that involved a rape and one other movie that my wife walked out on. In those three the rapes were not credible. Rape is the one subject that divides the human race in two. Most women, I learned, even up to a grandmotherly age, worry about rape from time to time. The only men who worry about rape are those isolated in prison. So outside of prison, the two sexes have greatly differing views. The research I did—a few conversations with men in the justice system concerned about rape cases and one woman who had been raped—corroborated that view. I was dumbstruck by the cavalier attitude of the men (times have changed; most educated men take rape seriously now, as does the law in some countries). The movies and TV had fashioned rape scenes that came across as "made up." How could I make the rape in the novel seem real and thereby be meaningful?

I decided to create a minor character, the rapist's wife, speaking in the first person. If I could make her credible, and we saw her husband through her eyes, the rapist might seem real, and therefore the rape might seem real. Hence the comment by Mary

Koslak, which appears just before the rape. Later, I added a chapter from the rapist's point of view. And several chapters from the point of view of Dr. Koch, a psychiatrist who showed up in *The Magician* and who succeeded in getting into this book also. It turns out that Francine, the rape victim, is his patient, and that the doctor is trying to deal with his own romantic feelings for his patient while trying to help her.

This multiple first-person form is a wonderfully useful technique for the novelist who accepts his role as an impersonator. It is an opportunity for the writer to re-create life, in which we all speak in the first person to each other. I have never been a sixty-year-old psychiatrist, a criminal lawyer, a WASP wife, a horse breeder, a rapist, or any of the other characters in the book, but how I enjoyed writing them! Out of the web of those characters came the story. I have to report that *Other People* earned my first five-star review, the most money I've ever made from a novel, and a blessing from Meryl Streep, who, within a week or two of publication, offered to play the role of Francine. (The three people I knew in Hollywood at the time all said she wasn't bankable!) I hope the success of *Other People* will encourage readers of this book to experiment with techniques that remain invisible to the reader yet reach the reader's emotions, such as the multiple first-person voices of this chapter.

NINE

Do You Promise to Tell the Truth, So Help You?

A writer cannot write what he does not read with pleasure. He must write what he most loves to read. I recognize that I am speaking to two tribes of writers. There is the line that descends from Shakespeare—sometimes descending far too much in its attempts to be literary. And there is the line that descends from Marlowe, the melodramatist from whom Shakespeare cribbed some plots before he learned that writing is a way of exploring human nature.

Much has been written about the line that descends from Shakespeare. Less has been written about the melodramas that descend from Marlowe. This book is addressed to both lines, to those who are trying to write a good book and those who are trying to write a good read. They are different occupations, but both can profit from knowledge of their craft.

Trapdoors and pitfalls exist in both occupations. The would-be writer of literary fiction sometimes slides into passivity and inconsequence no reader will follow for long. The writer of melodrama is sometimes in such a hurry to get his plot on paper that he neglects the development of interesting characters and credible actions. If the writer of melodrama also neglects precision in his use of language, he can easily stumble into hackwork.

It is important to understand how melodrama differs from genuine drama. Melodrama can be thought of as opera without the music. It may emphasize spectacle, exaggerated physical action, sensational violence, and extravagant emotion, which come off both on stage and in books as lacking in credibility. Melodrama flourished onstage in nineteenth-century plays and in early-twentieth-century films. Anyone who today sits through any of the early films, even the ones considered great by film buffs, knows what melodrama is, and why its incredulity leaves us uncomfortable when its object is not laughter. Melodrama is naive in its perception of human nature. There is a certain hypocrisy in melodramatic fiction. People do not behave in life as they do in those books. Heroes and heroines in melodrama are virtuous to an extreme. Villains are of unmitigated evil. We have learned since that heroes and heroines are more convincing when they are vulnerable, and villains more credible when they use charm as well as guile with their victims.

The stories that suffuse much thriller and mystery fiction cannot be looked at closely because they don't ring true, they are "made up" of actions often closer to cartoons than to life. Their stereotyped heroes and villains are propelled by motives and emotions that seem spurious or sentimental. Characterization in melodrama is anything but subtle. Instead of the rounded characters of fiction who live on in memory, the characters of melodrama are maneuvered like puppets to suit the turns of a plot usually too far-fetched to be considered anything but entertainment of a transient kind. Melodrama attracts huge audiences who do not look to books for insight or the pleasures of language, and who are content with diversion. The reader eagerly suspends disbelief and goes for the ride. When he is through, the reader puts the book aside and may never think of it again. Melodrama does not provide the reader with an understanding of human nature, or with lingering memories of characters after their stories have been put away. It thrives on exaggerated or pseudo-emotion. Jean Cocteau referred to it as "sentimental blackmail." That said, melodrama in book form, so often called "commercial fiction," is a transient form of fiction that in each publishing season makes some writers rich.

Writers who have never developed a love of character and language and whose reading is confined to thrillerdom are not likely candidates for writing anything else. Those thriller readers who turn to writing, I counsel to perfect their craft, to try to create characters that are credible and whose actions can be believed.

The writers of literary fiction accept a different responsibility. They skate on ice that is as thin as the paper on which their words appear. They are undertaking through realism or fantasy to deal with their perceptions of truth, to re-create life on the page. When they do their best work, it may affect large numbers of people beyond the writer's lifetime. Their perceptions about some human situation may pass as part of culture and be witnessed by people in future generations. To knowingly lie to future generations somehow seems a great sin.

That speaks to the writer's moral obligation. Having created experiences that are perceived as true, especially those that resonate in memory, the writer, though he invents as well as discovers, and lets his imagination take him and his readers to places he may never have visited in life, has an obligation not to distort his insight about the conduct of human beings.

The writer of serious fiction has the same worry as a criminal. Do your work ineptly and you will be caught and put away, out of sight, by critics and readers. Erica Jong, the author of *Fear of Fly-*

ing, learned early that you can make it as a writer "if you are relentlessly honest about what you feel and fear." Writing serious fiction is dangerous, exhilarating, and vastly rewarding.

Shakespeare gave us more truths about human behavior than we have had from any wise man since. His predecessor, Marlowe, gave us melodrama that is rarely read or performed. Each writer would like to think he has a chance to choose his professional ancestors. I am here to say that by what you read with pleasure, you have already chosen. Now do your best.

TEN

Where Writers Go Wrong

I am going to take you into the privacy of my editorial room and let you eavesdrop on the editorial suggestions I made to two writers of differing backgrounds, with different intentions, both with full novels in draft. Imagine yourself looking over my shoulder as we proceed.

The first author is an experienced teacher of writing in a distinguished college who is struggling with her own first work of full-length fiction. I took her on after reading some of her published nonfiction work, which is excellent. I will tell you what is right and wrong with her manuscript, and the plan I gave her for fixing it. You may find elements of that plan helpful in your own work.

Her manuscript is a long historical novel. The story rambles without a clear focus. The writing is overly rich; its adjectives, similes, and metaphors come too frequently, making the reader aware of the writing instead of letting him experience the story.

To straighten out the rambling plot, I advised her to tell me the story as simply as possible in less than one page. All of the most successful novels I have edited over the years have had stories that could be synopsized in a single paragraph.

Her second assignment was to break that story into scenes. In the first chapter of this book I explain how that is done. It saves a great deal of time if the scene outline is done before the draft is written, but in this case it had to be done afterward.

I asked for a list of those scenes in the order in which they were to appear in the novel. My intention was to see which scenes were best, which were below par and might be eliminated, and to try to eliminate as much as possible of the narrative summary between scenes.

I asked the author to tell me what she hoped the reader would feel during each scene, keeping in mind that the main task of fiction is to give the reader a continuing emotional experience. We looked at this scene list together to see if the order seemed right, and to see if any weak scenes were really necessary.

The novel in question had two protagonists, which is a bit like having two wives or two husbands. Can loyalty or affection be divided fairly? I strongly oppose having more than one protagonist because the reader's emotions become diffused. If a writer has difficulty deciding who is the main character, he should ask himself which character's experience is the stronger in this story, or which character undergoes the greatest change that exemplifies the story.

I recall a California writer who had a novel-in-progress with three protagonists. It didn't work. When she finally figured out which of the three women was the one she would focus on, the novel came to life. In the case of the historical novelist, I asked her to settle on one protagonist. I had a good idea who that protagonist should be, but I kept mum. I wanted to see what she decided because her self-questioning about the protagonist would help her clarify the story she had in mind. The process of finding out *whose story it is* can become an important learning adventure for the writer.

After she settled on the protagonist, I asked her to look at her scene list. Ideally, the protagonist should play an important role in the first scene to avoid the reader mistaking another character for the protagonist. One of the marks of amateur novel-writing is a lack of early clarity as to whose story we, as readers, should be following. If the reader misjudges and finds out down the line that it is really someone else's story, the reader will not appreciate the change.

The writer and I discussed her rewrite of the first chapter, which was a big improvement over an earlier version. However, there were still a number of faults to be remedied. They are listed here only to suggest the kind of matters all writers should be sensitive to.

The first and second sentences had to have their order reversed in order to help the reader know what he was looking at as the author set the scene.

I recommended deleting sentences or parts of sentences that conveyed information that the reader already knew. I also recommended breaking up long sentences, which increases pace and tension.

The author used self-conscious asides that disrupted the reader's experience. I suggested she delete them.

I placed brackets around many adjectives that needed deletion. In each case the deletion strengthened the sentence.

I urged the elimination of melodrama, where the action was excessive and lacked credibility.

I noted author intrusions; that is, places where only the author could have known what was said. The author—unless he or she is a narrator—doesn't belong in the story.

I questioned whether one minor character should appear at the beginning. That character's later appearance in the first chapter would come as a strong surprise if the earlier, unimportant appearance was eliminated.

I suggested certain fixes in dialogue. For instance, "Her voice dropped to a whisper" should appear before the whispered words, not after.

What you have above are about half of the suggestions I made for corrections in the improved first chapter. That will indicate the amount as well as the kind of editing that often takes place in professional work with talented and experienced writers who have not yet published fiction.

The second example is the work of a successful senior lawyer, not yet retired, but taking more and more time for his creative writing, which he enjoys far more than the legal writing he has been doing all his life. His enjoyment is palpable, which made him interesting as a prospective client. More important, however, was the fact that his manuscript, a thriller, has a central character who is not only credible but lovable. Also, the faults of the story, while many, were fixable. In a trial run of just one chapter, I found him responsive and able to use suggestions to fix problems and enhance the characterization of the other characters, as well as to improve the readability of the text. All of this augured well for eventual publication if he could keep up the level of improvement over the length of a novel. He was astonished to find how complex the craft of fiction writing is (true of many writers who come from successful careers in other professions), but he learned with the enthusiasm that makes the editor's work worthwhile.

In the first draft that I saw, it was unclear in the early pages who the protagonist was. A new president is about to be inaugurated. The protagonist is a member of the outgoing cabinet, who has no lasting interest in politics and can't wait to get back home. To get the story moving, one sentence was suggested. "This was their inauguration, not his." That thought did the trick and replaced paragraphs of unclear material.

I ask writers to insure that there is something visual on each page. In the original, the garroting of the secretary of defense was an offstage event, conveyed to the reader in narrative summary. It is now a scene that is witnessed.

In fiction the writer has to be careful not to deliver nonfiction messages about controversial issues. The manuscript addressed racism as an issue that was not central to the story, and when first dealt with seemed heavy-handed and inappropriate. The author rethought it, and after a couple of tries came up with a few credible lines of dialogue that did the job to replace what seemed like an authorial exhortation.

The early part of the book contained a lot of unnecessary words that softened the pace. When they were bracketed and later removed by the author, the pace quickened. Cliches were improved or eliminated. A badgering reporter was portrayed unrealistically. All that was fixed by the author. What was not fixed till a later draft was the catastrophic explosion that propels the story into focus. The explosion was described, not shown. It had to be redone with convincing detail as if the reader were watching the explosion happen.

The book has two major villains, both high-powered government officials. Both portrayals came across as cartoons rather than people. The effect was to make their opposition to the protagonist not credible, and the ensuing conflict sound made up rather than a story that could be experienced by the reader in tense scenes. One of these characters is in a hotel room with an expensive prostitute and catches the explosion on TV while the woman does her nails. In revision, the author turned this into an amusing and credible sequence by reducing the melodramatic villainy of the character.

Many authors new to fiction have trouble with "beats." A beat is usually a minor action that breaks up dialogue when a pause is needed to keep the scene visual. In times past this was accomplished by the lighting of a cigarette or the sipping of a drink. Both of these actions quickly became cliche, and are now the mark of a careless writer. I encouraged the author to replace cliche beats with some credible and appropriate small actions that provided a pause in the dialogue.

Toward the end of the first chapter the author delivered, in flashback, a lecture about the protagonist's background and beliefs that would have seriously damaged the reader's interest. The story stopped while this background was provided. The reader's experience of the story evaporated. Once this was pointed out, the author was able to condense this wordy background into two well-crafted, convincing sentences, all that was needed.

The point of view needed to be fixed in a scene in which a killing takes place. Point of view requires tight discipline. It also requires consistency, or it results in a loss of authorial control that throws the reader off. The usual advice is to try to use the point of view of the person most affected by what is happening. In a killing, the person most affected is the victim. In a third-person point-of-view story, the victim's point of view is acceptable as long as it doesn't continue beyond loss of consciousness or death! I pointed out how the victim's point of view might be sustained during the attack.

> The intruder's knee slammed into the small of Fred's back, pushing his face into the wall. Something thin and metal pressed into his neck. He tried to turn. He tried to shout, as he felt the garrote tighten. Fred clawed at his neck, his arms flailed, as he tried to reach his unseen assailant. He kicked and twisted. He couldn't breathe. *Who would want to kill me?*

Preserving a single point of view is crucial in scenes of great moment. In this case, it should be the victim's up to the point of his choking, and then shift to the killer.

The author introduced some "burly FBI agents" as heavies, replete with trench coats and close-cropped hair. Not only were they cartoonish cliches, but their appearance also destroyed the credibility of the scenes they were in. FBI agents, policemen, detectives, all should be characterized as one would characterize people in other professions, with individual particularity, and played straight.

Chapter three of the author's manuscript gave me a bit of a worry because on first reading I was unsure at this point in the story who the real antagonist was. I discussed this with the author, who had several characters in mind as antagonists, thus diffusing their effect. In conversation it became clear who the most important antagonist was. Clarifying his role in the novel required a rewriting of his appearances. It is a common occurrence that a new fiction writer will make the villain too villainous, and that was true in this case also. My radical suggestion had the writer thinking of the protagonist and the antagonist as *two antagonists*, each of whom should be given his due. It makes for more-credible conflict and a better story.

The author used two pet dogs early in the plot. At first glance I thought they might be an unnecessary diversion, but on reflection I found that the protagonist's appreciation of the dogs and concern for them humanized him. The dogs stayed.

In one place the author used a long excerpt from a statute book. When we talked about it, it was clear to him as well as to me that it was a reflex from his many years of legal writing and had no place in this fiction except as a brief reference in colloquial dialogue.

A small point: I often see awkward choices of names for characters. The author used Silvia and Silver, which were too similar. Silver is the last name of the protagonist. I suggested changing the other name. It's even a good idea to avoid giving two important characters names that start with the same letter. The reader speeding ahead will have to slow down to register the right character. It's best to avoid any confusion or distraction that will divert the reader from his experience.

While it can be an advantage to refer to well-known people by name in a novel, singular names of real people should not be given to characters invented by the author. In this manuscript, the author used names that were too obviously reminiscent of either actual persons (e.g., Thurgood, Kareem Hassan Jabal) or too indicative of how the author feels about the character (e.g., Blaggart; Blagg would be okay).

I marked a passage in narrative summary that was easily convertible to dialogue. That turned the retelling of an offstage event into a visible scene. Dialogue is always "immediate scene."

The next-to-last paragraph of the first chapter of this writer's manuscript was a perfect chapter ending, spoiled by an additional paragraph. A chapter ending should thrust the reader into the next chapter, usually by raising a question that is not answered. The author cut the additional paragraph and thereby improved the book in an important place.

I marked a number of spots in which clauses needed to be transposed. This common flaw is covered in the next chapter of this book.

Phone conversations in fiction are not replicas of phone conversations in life. They are considerably foreshortened versions that serve the necessity of the story. They should not be used often. If an author hopes that his novel will be bought for film, phone conversations should be used sparingly or not at all because they can be a problem for the screenwriter. In the case of this author, I questioned the need of a particular phone conversation.

I pointed out that in a scene that should be tense, there was too much about fishing. The reader knows that an assassin is watching the fisherman. The fishing details needed to be trimmed down to preserve the tension of the scene.

When I mark "We know" in a manuscript, it means that the author is providing information that the reader already knows. "We know" passages should always be cut.

The author had five sentences in a row that began with "He . . ." Substitutes needed to be found for some of them.

The author referred to a "small black car." Particularity helps enhance the reality of a scene. I suggested calling the car by its make and kind.

I also suggested a place where the author might add an omen, a portent of something to come. An "omen" should not be confused with "telegraphing," which is less subtle and tells the reader of a future event before it happens.

I pointed out that too many characters were smiling too often. Head shaking was also overused.

The finding of bodies of important people is not something that should be told about as a throwaway. I recommended a realistic scene that the reader could witness.

I pointed out good plot points so that the author would have a measure of his own creation for the improvement of other plot points.

In a later chapter, I was put off by a discussion. Discussions are seldom useful in fiction. Confrontations are. Arguments are. I once edited a novel by an eminent doctor that included meetings in which doctors discussed cases and administration, as they do in life. It was boring. If what happens at a meeting is necessary to the story, zoom in on that moment and leave the rest of the meeting out. Readers do not enjoy transcripts even if abbreviated.

In going over the early chapters a second time, I recommended that the author had too many modifiers for some nouns. Stripped of the excess, the sentences became stronger.

Choice of words is, of course, of maximum importance. In the tense first chapter, I was stopped twice by a door that was "already opened." The "already" throws the reader into a momentary time switch that is distracting. "Unlocked" or "open" would avoid the problem.

At a place where the action was confusing, I suggested the author think of himself with a hand-held camera, and show what the camera would see in sequence. That usually clears up the problem.

I cautioned the author to avoid sentences like "It was John Smith . . ." Unless it is a thought of a character within that character's point of view, only the author could be saying that. The author belongs at the computer, not among the characters in the book.

In a scene that takes place after sex, the author had a generalization, with the character "thinking about doing it again." I suggested replacing that with the man seeing something sexy belonging to the woman that makes him think of "the next time."

I pointed to a line of dialogue that was too logical for the character speaking.

Because of a reference to a college course taken by a character, I worried out loud about the age of that character for his role in the novel. The reference to the college course, it turned out, had to be eliminated. This kind of thing is usually caught by the copy editor after the manuscript is accepted. I try to get authors to clean up these small points ahead of time because their negative effect is cumulative.

The author had someone *sprinting* across an office. That's pretty hard to do even in a large office. "Sprinting" had to be replaced by a more accurate word.

In one action, a TV news helicopter was hovering over a crime scene and interfering with a law-enforcement helicopter trying to take off. When the crew of the news helicopter failed to respond immediately to a radioed order from the lawmen on the ground, a senior lawman fired a burst into the air to scare off the TV news helicopter. This seemed melodramatic and not credible. The lawman's order, "If you impede us, you will be shot down," seemed sufficient to get the TV news people moving out of the way.

I complimented the writer on the way he handled a particular half page that made the reader want to cheer the protagonist. That's helpful to the reader. What's helpful to the writer is having someone else, in this case the editor, pointing out the skillful things that work because the writer can use such instances as models for his other work.

The writer knows the names of the characters much better than any reader will. In one section a character was described as having a "shock of prematurely white hair," but he was not named. That jars the reader. It's easy to get a character's name in, especially in dialogue.

A piece of formal-sounding writing crept in. I suggested a simple, colloquial substitute: "The ball is yours." That carried the full import of the formal-sounding speech.

I pointed to a place where the writer had said the same thing in two different ways. This is a common error. You may recall my formula: one plus one equals a half. That formula is designed to remind writers that conveying the same matter more than once in different words diminishes the effect of what is said. Either way alone would have a stronger effect.

Quotes are for spoken dialogue, not for thoughts. If the point of view is firmly established in the character, one doesn't need to say "he thought" to introduce a thought. Just do it. For example:

Was he up to it? How would this affect Jane? And what about the girls?

If the point of view is from the person thinking, the reader will understand that these are his thoughts. The context, of course, helps.

I marked a speech by the antagonist as too bald and offensive. In addition, this villain's physical description was overloaded. The character was described as "Greasy, scars, reeking," with a "stained tie" and "beer gut." I urged the author to make that character look good, making his opposition to the hero more effective. Ugly, slovenly villains are a Hollywood cliche. Realistically portrayed, strong villains make for stronger stories.

I urged the author to keep thinking of his hero and chief villain as two antagonists rather than hero and villain so that the contest between them would not be a foregone conclusion. The better the villain, the greater the contest and the hero's victory.

I would add only that several days later I received the author's revised pages, and they brought pleasure to the editor's heart. An editor's work is designed to help the writer realize the writer's intentions, and in this case the improvement in the execution was a rewarding experience. If the author keeps up the level of improvement, this book has a chance of becoming his first published novel.

ELEVEN

How to Pilot Words Precisely

You are about to take a trip in an airline I won't name. If the door leading to the cockpit were open, you'd see the pilot in the left seat preparing for takeoff. He jiggles the control on an instrument to his right front, setting it first to seventy-one, then changing his mind and setting it to seventy-three. When he gets an odd look from the copilot, he turns it back to seventy-one. He flips switches one, two, three, top to bottom, gets another look from the copilot, and flips switch two back down. This occasions an even dirtier look from the copilot, who is seventeen years younger and too outspoken, though he hasn't said a word. "Okay, okay," the pilot says, and flips up switch two and flips switch three to its original position. The copilot acknowledges the correction with a profound sigh. Finished with the switches, the pilot opens his mike to the cabin and announces, "Prepare for takeoff." This time the copilot can't restrain himself and says, "Jack, we're still connected to the jetway! Would you like me to drive this trip?"

Would you like to be aboard that airplane? Would you rather be in a plane on which the pilot followed a checklist or knew it accurately by heart? How many times have you picked up a novel and within pages wondered what the hell the author was doing? Instead of being involved in the experience of the story, you were bumping into murky writing, misplaced clauses, the incorrect use of words. Fortunately for those of us who travel, pilots seem to make far fewer errors than writers who force their readers to puzzle out meanings.

If the reader picks up a book, his preference is for an author who knows what he is doing every step of the way instead of making him reread sentences. If there are enough glitches, the reader isn't going to spend twelve hours on your trip. He'll toss your book and pick up another by a writer who's been careful.

Talented and smart writers, concentrating on their characters and story, are sometimes bothered by an editor's attention to glitches in their handling of language. In his autobiography, Elia Kazan said,

> Anything I'd learned about editing films didn't help me edit a book, particularly if it was my own. Stein took charge of me; he had to. He would ask, then suggest, later insist, and finally proceed ruthlessly (so I thought) to cut out chunks of the book. . . . He seemed to relish looping paragraphs in red ink, then transferring them, by the continuation of the red line, to another location in my text. My pages became a battleground after the battle; he'd violated them with lines, scratches, arrows, circles and curves and great wasted gaps.

I plead guilty. Luckily, Kazan had a top-notch secretary who deciphered all my transpositions and typed a clean copy for him to work on. Today, working on a computer, revisions are a relative snap. Authors complain a lot less about my transpositions—or their own, once they learn to look for glitches in their early drafts.

The single most common mistake I find in the manuscripts I edit, including the work of professionals, are words, phrases, clauses, sentences, and paragraphs in the wrong order. When a writer puts down the material that flows from the top of his mind, it's difficult for him to judge whether everything is in the right order. With practice, the out-of-order parts can be spotted in revision and changed.

What do I mean by the wrong order? Let's look at a tiny example that merely slows the text down. ("Merely" is probably the wrong word when you're working on a book that you hope will succeed.) I am looking at the weathered draft manuscript of what became a number-one bestseller. On the second page of Kazan's manuscript of *The Arrangement* I saw, "Florence, my wife, and I were the envy of every other married couple in Beverly Hills and Bradshaw Park." The commas after Florence and after wife slow the reader. It was easily transposed to read, "My wife Florence and I . . ." Time and again, I have heard writers say, "I leave that stuff to copy editors," or words to that effect. My view is that the first reader you are slowing down is the editor considering whether to buy your book!

Let's look at another example. "When she came in, she'd latch the door and lock it . . ." Why not just "lock the door"? That eliminates half the words and with a simple transposition eliminates flab, the excessive words that weaken a sentence.

Sometimes these small transpositions increase the impact of a sentence. For instance, Eddie, the hero of Kazan's novel, is talking about the early development of his bond with his wife. In the original, he said, "I was a mess when she met me, crouched down in my little burrow, my legs drawn up under me, ready to spring or snap, eyes frantic, teeth bared and ready." I made one inconsequential change, "spring and snap" instead of "spring or snap," because the "or" gave the reader a split-second choice instead of a continuous action. To make a strong sentence stronger, I transposed the frantic eyes to the end of the sentence, so that it read, "I was a mess when she met me, crouched down in my little burrow, my legs drawn up under me, ready to spring and snap, teeth bared and ready, eyes frantic." The readiness of the character to spring and snap, teeth bared, is aggressive. The eyes frantic conveys the character's own terror, making him aggressive because he is frightened, a much stronger point.

I suggested many hundreds of such changes in each draft, and each draft, with the author's reluctant acknowledgment, became stronger. Learning to put phrases, clauses, sentences, and paragraphs into a better order for achieving an emotional effect on the reader is a necessary part of the writer's craft.

Do I make the same mistakes? Every author does the first time around, which is why Hemingway said all first drafts are excrement. I just noticed a needed transposition in another chapter of the book you are holding in your hands. I had a sentence that read, "Similarly, we try to avoid shouting in life." I cut the "Similarly" as an unneeded word, then transposed the next five words with the last two, so that the sentence now reads, "In life we try to avoid shouting," which puts the emphasis in the right place.

Here's another example from a later chapter of this book.

> A writer feels a hollowness, an absence, a longing on those days when circumstances outside himself prevent his writing.

I transposed the clauses. Here is the improved result.

> On those days when circumstances outside himself prevent the writer from writing, he feels a hollowness, an absence, a longing.

In Kazan's autobiography, *A Life*, he refers to a formula, "one plus one equals a half," a formula I designed to remind writers that conveying the same matter more than once in different words diminishes the effect of what is said. Kazan had one of those on the second page of his manuscript.

> I knew I had to give Gwen up. I knew the moment was on me, that moment when you can still quit and walk away free and clear, without lasting injury to either side, and just before that other moment when somebody's going to get hurt.

Can you find the one plus one, the words that aren't necessary because they repeat what other words say? It isn't "moment" because the repetition of that word lends desirable emphasis. It's the words "quit and." "I knew the moment was on me, that moment when you can still walk away" implies the "quit" without ambiguity.

> I knew I had to give Gwen up. I knew the moment was on me, that moment when you can still walk away free and clear, without lasting injustice to either side, and just before that other moment when somebody's going to get hurt.

If you think that's too small a matter to bother correcting, why are you so concerned about the pilot who was lax about the switches? Because your life was in danger? Believe me, your manuscript is equally in danger if you overlook these seemingly small things. Given the attitude in the publishing industry toward the cost of what once used to be normal editing work, it behooves the author to eliminate these glitches on his own.

In fiction, I frequently question the order of whole paragraphs and sections. At the moment I am editing the work of an accomplished nonfiction writer, the author of books you may have read and movies you may have seen. I am on the page of his manuscript in which he is describing how his passion for a certain food saved his life. Had he eaten less and got to his destination earlier, he would have been blown up in one of history's worst terrorist explosions. He witnessed the wreckage and hurried to the radio station to broadcast the first eyewitness account of the explosion. On the way he was detained by a soldier, but managed to get away in time to make his historic broadcast. What's wrong?

The order in which he put the material: He tells about the huge bomb going off first, then about seeing the wreckage, getting stopped by the soldier, getting to the radio station barely on time, then an aside about a journalist friend who disappeared in a different country, then back to broadcasting the first eyewitness account, and then the fact that he missed being blown up himself by minutes because he was lingering over a favorite food. To keep material like that suspenseful, the author needed to arrange the events *in chronological order as he experienced them so that we, the readers, can experience the tension of the events as they happened to him.* The reader, interestingly enough, is more forgiving if in nonfiction the facts are in the wrong order, as long as he gets the facts. In fiction, if the reader has to figure out the order of events, suspense and tension are eliminated. The experience has been muddled to the reader's—and writer's—disadvantage.

Let us consider the description of an action presented in the wrong order. I have found errors of this sort more frequently than you'd imagine in the manuscripts of some famously successful authors. Fortunately, editors and copy editors will catch most of these, but it is useful to remember that the editor, like the agent, is a *reader*, and that you want both agent and editor to see a manuscript that is as glitch-proof as possible.

Readers, however fast they read, perceive actions sequentially. Students of German know how frustrating that language can be because the reader is frequently hung up on meaning until he gets to the verb at the end of the sentence. Let's examine an out-of-sequence sentence.

"Crossing Madison Avenue, Henry was hit by a speeding bicycle driven by one of those New York City messengers who don't pay attention to red lights and suddenly dart out between cars at pedestrians who are crossing on the Walk signal."

That's a clumsy, run-on sentence. If the point of view is Henry's, the reader needs Henry to see the Walk signal, notice that the cars have really stopped for the red light, start to cross, and suddenly get hit by a messenger's bicycle. There are a number of ways of doing this correctly. If the action is in any way complex, break it up into shorter sentences. Here's one way of doing it:

"Henry waited on the sidewalk for the Don't Walk sign to change. When it did, he waited till all the cars at the intersection had come to a full stop, then started across Madison Avenue, only to glimpse one of those bike-riding messengers zipping out between stopped cars straight at him."

Note how the point of view remains Henry's. Note also that the action is described in a sequence that doesn't require the reader to figure things out. It is visual. The correct order preserves the reader's involvement in the story.

Warning: In nonfiction, and especially in academic writing, the words "former" and "latter" are used to designate which of two things just said applies. I caution nonfiction writers who want to be read rather than studied to avoid the use of "former" and "latter" because when the reader encounters those words, he often has to momentarily backtrack for understanding. It is a lazy way of writing; there is always some way of reorganizing the thought to avoid bobbing the reader's attention back and forth.

Footnotes are also glitches, whether at the bottom of the page or in back of the book. If footnotes are a scholarly requirement, take a look at Bertram D. Wolfe's masterpiece, *Three Who Made a Revolution*, and see how you know his source from the text, obviating the need for footnotes. Of course, if you're writing a paper not for the general reader but to fulfill an academic requirement, your few readers may not trust your work unless you display all of your footnotes prominently.

The point of all of my suggestions that pertain to the novelist is to minimize the reader's effort to experience the story. The purpose of eliminating glitches in nonfiction is to enable the reader to grasp meaning *as he reads*. It takes work on the writer's part, but the less work the reader has to do, the better will be his appreciation of what the writer has done.

Let's get back in that airplane for a moment. When the pilot's voice on the intercom announces rough weather ahead and warns passengers to get back to their seats and buckle up, it is not only the pilot's words that count, but the authority of his voice as well. A pilot with a squeaky, nasal, hesitant, hoarse, or pontificating voice is not reassuring to the passenger. A pilot with a relaxed, natural-sounding voice makes us feel that there's a live individual we can trust up there in the cockpit. We especially enjoy a pilot's voice that has a touch of humor and that doesn't sound like he's regurgitating a memorized script. Similarly, the author's voice in a book makes an impression—good or bad—on the reader. Sometimes that voice sounds like somebody else's.

One of the better independent editors tells me that a problem she encounters among beginning fiction writers—even those with literary savvy—is that she has to help them find their voices so that the writing sounds like them and not offshoots of Danielle Steele or Dean Koontz. What to do?

First, let's understand what "voice" means. The term is defined in the glossary at the back of this book. Let me spare you the trouble of leaving this page by repeating the definition here. The author's voice is an amalgam of the many factors that distinguish a writer from all other writers. Many authors first find their voice when they have learned to examine each word for its necessity, precision, and clarity, and have become expert in eliminating the extraneous and imprecise from their work. A writer's voice is strengthened when he is able to say what he really thinks without the restraint of what someone else will think about it. The voice is also strengthened when the author, in his attempt to be writerly, comes up with fresh similes and metaphors that seem accurate and interesting to the reader. Recognizing an individual author's voice is much like recognizing a person's voice on the telephone.

Is there a shortcut for a writer finding his or her own voice? Cutting out all the cliches helps. Keeping things visual also helps. Here's a technique you can try that enables a writer to get rid of any of the formality or posturing that creeps into the early drafts of fiction: Talk the first page of your story into an audiocassette machine without looking at your text, as if your audience is one person, your closest friend. Don't censor. Use colloquialisms, expletives if you have to, anything that first comes to mind in conveying the story. Don't worry about run-on sentences, punctuation, paragraphing; just talk. Then type out what you've said on tape. Try this several times with different short sections of what you're writing, and you may find your voice a lot sooner.

TWELVE

You Have All the Time You Need

I would like to remind you of a definition I put before you in the preface: A writer is someone who cannot not write.

If you're determined to write, the question is when do you write? Obviously, when you can. I had a student once who did her writing standing up in the kitchen attending pots on the stove. Ideally, one ought to write in a place and at a time when the chances of being disturbed are minimal. Writing fiction is often like juggling ideas the way a juggler keeps balls in the air. An interruption can be hazardous to the health of the interrupter, or to a good sentence that escapes uncaptured.

It is equally advantageous to write at the same time every day. Our bodily mechanisms learn to cooperate. Writers with a morning metabolism are best off writing first thing, even if it means getting up earlier than one might otherwise. Late-night writers find their most productive time when other people are asleep. But larks and night-owls alike will find that if they write at the same hour regularly, the work will come easier as they develop their skill, particularly if they leave off writing when the going is still good, jotting down whatever it is they need to remember for start-up the next time.

Yes, there are conditions that make it next to impossible to write, for instance in the early weeks of a child's life when its parents are likely to be sleep deprived. Or during illness. Or on traveling vacations, though a lightweight laptop can be tempting.

I know the problems. For twenty-seven years I headed a book-publishing firm that turned out an average of a hundred titles a year, yet during that time I wrote nine published novels, and much else. When writers complained to me that this or that prevented them from writing, I cited an author of mine named Christy Brown, the most disadvantaged writer in the history of the world. You may have heard of him in connection with the movie made of his life, *My Left Foot.* Christy, author of five books, including the bestselling novel *Down All the Days*, had only the use of the little toe on his left foot. He wrote his manuscripts one letter at a time on a special typewriter IBM contrived for him. All the lines on the occasional letter I received from Christy slid upwards at an acute angle because IBM didn't figure out how to make the paper-grip work on the special typewriter. Christy wrote his three novels and two books of poetry within a single decade, taking time off to do the *Today Show* and the *David Frost Show* and interviews in England, all from the wheelchair he was confined to for life. What did you say your problem was?

THIRTEEN

Revision as Opportunity—and Danger

An editor I care for gave me *The Complete Stories* of Bernard Malamud, a Christmas present that caused me to put aside the other books I was reading. Malamud, the winner of many writing awards, including the Gold Medal for Fiction of the American Academy of Arts and Letters, once said that writers who do only one draft are cheating themselves. "First drafts," he went on, "are for learning what your novel or story is about. Revision is working with that knowledge to enlarge and enhance an idea, to re-form it. D. H. Lawrence," Malamud pointed out, "did seven or eight drafts of *The Rainbow*. The first draft of a book is the most uncertain—where you need guts, the ability to accept the imperfect until it is better. Revision," he added, "is one of the true pleasures of writing."

John Fowles completed the first draft of his early breakthrough novel, *The Collector*, in under a month, writing as much as ten thousand words in a day. He said, "Of course a lot of it was poorly written and had to be endlessly amended and revised. First-draft and revision writing are so different they hardly seem to belong to the same activity. I never do any 'research' until the first draft is finished; all that matters to begin with is the flow, the story, the narrating. Having research material then is like swimming in a straitjacket."

Fowles rushed his writing as if in a fever to get his story down, but before you jump to a conclusion, give him a moment more: "During the revision period I try to keep some sort of discipline. I make myself revise whether I feel like it or not; in some ways, the more disinclined and dyspeptic one feels, the better—one is harsher with oneself. All the best cutting is done when one is sick of the writing."

I've offered the views of Malamud and Fowles, two brilliant second-half-of-the-twentieth-century writers who are greatly different from each other, because so many newcomers to fiction have a cockeyed view of the writing process. I occasionally hear, as I did just a week before writing this chapter, from an as-yet-unpublished fiction writer who is absolutely sure that the draft he would like to put before me is going to knock agents and editors dead. Writers so certain of their early drafts—the word that comes to mind is *unprofessional*—almost always require more editorial work than I'm willing to give to someone wearing armor and a halo. Fortunately, among my clients are those who can't wait to get editorial notes, as if their happiness and future depended on the continuation of their work. It is always a pleasure to work with them. Even experienced and successful professionals sometimes slip up badly. What makes them a pleasure to work with is that after the sometimes painful shock of a professional critique of an early draft, they recover quickly and get to work.

Leslie Fiedler, an honored critic whose works about other writers graced the front cover of *The New York Times Book Review* more than once, knows more about writing than most of us. On one occasion he drove eight hours from Buffalo to my home to go over in person my comments on his then-newest novel. Our meeting was touchy. My comment about his novel was brief. I said, "Leslie, your novel starts on page 129." He did not seem happy. Behind the momentary flush and shock in his expression lay the months of work he'd spent on pages 1 through 128. He asked if I had an open bottle of bourbon and a tumbler. I supplied them. He took them and his manuscript to the desk in the library of my home, and disappeared for hours. When he finally emerged, his comment to me was as brief as mine had been to him. "You're right," he said. I joined him in a toast to his next draft, which came out fine, and which I published gladly.

On another occasion, Elia Kazan came to me with the manuscript of his third book, the first two having been enormously successful. "This time," he said, "tell me everything at once." I studied the manuscript with care and supplied him with quite a few pages of typed notes along with marginal markings in the manuscript. Some weeks later he returned with a revised draft. We were on the stone promenade outside my living room when I said I had quite a few additional comments for him. "What?!" was his response as he stepped closer and put his hands around my throat. "I asked you to tell me everything the first time!"

When his temper simmered down enough for us to sit in the sun side by side, I told him that if I had given him *all* my comments at once, he might have tossed the manuscript away in despair. So despite his injunction to "tell me all," I divided my comments into two workable groups. That's a judgment as to how much a writer can take at one time. If you're working without an editor, you might find that your own critique of a draft is too much to take. The remedy could be the same: Make the most important changes, create a new draft, and work that over with an editorial eye to see what still needs fixing.

I received a phone call recently from a writer who didn't sound like anyone who needed editorial help. His previous novel had sold over four million copies, was made into a successful movie, and had something like eighty-five printings in paperback. His new book was nonfiction. He told me it hadn't been seen by anyone, he was nervous about its reception (nervous? four million copies?), and would I give him an appraisal. I told him I was finishing a novel and this book, and was not taking on any new clients until I finished both. This author, it happens, is an astute salesman. The next day the manuscript arrived at my doorstep via Federal Express. With it came an inscribed copy of his four-million-copy seller. I settled into a comfortable chair to read.

A couple of days later I faxed him a five-page, single-spaced memorandum for revision, not what he expected and not what I had anticipated. Much of the first half of the book had to be scrapped. In the excellent second half were all the clues for what should have been done in the first half. The next thing I heard from him was that he was staying up till four in the morning rewriting, on a high, on a roll, and excited about what he was doing. That is a professional, a man who has been writing, editing, and publishing his work for decades. I suspect that a less experienced writer, seeing my five-page single-spaced memorandum, might have hunted down another editor who might have let him get away easier.

Years ago, when I was a book publisher, an agent gave me first offer of a novel by a writer using the pseudonym of Oliver Lange. The condition was that I read the manuscript myself and that I read it that night (it would arrive by messenger). I agreed to read it myself, but asked for two nights since I was hosting a party that evening. Two days later I called the agent, asked him what he wanted for the book, he named a price, I agreed, and then I got the bad news. The author, a former *New Yorker* writer, had moved to the mountains outside Santa Fe, where he lived with a wife and three children, no running water, and the nearest phone eight miles away, plus he didn't want to listen to what any editor had to say. In other words, the author didn't want to hear about any possible revising he might have to do.

The novel, in my opinion, was brilliant, but had one section that drooped. It needed serious tightening. Either the author did the fixing or somebody else would, but what was there now spoiled the book, and it was too good to be spoiled. It took a lot of doing by the agent to get the reluctant author into his Volkswagen and on his way to New York. When he arrived, we settled in my small study, a stone hideaway with glass on three sides looking out onto the surrounding greenery. Lange sat down in my typing chair (this was in pre-computer days) and swiveled toward me. "Shoot."

I talked to him for a couple of minutes about the section that dragged and what might be done to save it. He said, in effect, "Is that all?" He turned toward my typewriter, put a sheet of blank paper in, and told me to get lost.

From time to time I could hear him typing away. When he finished and shoved the pages at me, I saw they were now perfect. Lange asked for a bottle of wine. When my wife provided it, he said, "With the cork out," and then with the wine bottle in one hand, he waved good-bye with the other, and took off in his Volkswagen. The novel, called *Vandenberg* and in a later edition retitled *Defiance*, was selected by the Book-of-the-Month Club, had a six-figure paperback sale, a movie option, and made *The New York Times* bestseller list.

Some writers view a first draft as a holy object to be preserved from desecration. Desecration, yes, but revision is quite another matter. By now you should know that Hemingway was right when he said that all first drafts are excrement. *Revision is the most essential part of writing even for geniuses.* What we first put down is a document destined for change, and intended to be viewed with a jaundiced eye. Most professionals I know are embarrassed by their first drafts and can't wait to revise them because every new draft is an opportunity for improvement. The inexperienced writer may start revising immediately on completing a draft, to which I say, "Hold your horses!" You have not allowed some time to give you perspective, meaning objectivity and the chance to view what you have done as a reader rather than as the writer.

What if you have a deadline? What if you're being rushed to turn in a manuscript or have some other important reason to skip the waiting period for gaining objectivity? Fiction should not be written to deadline, but if you can't put a draft aside long enough to gain the objectivity of distance, there is something else you can do. Objectivity can also be gained by viewing your work in a medium different from the one in which it was composed. For instance, if you created your draft on computer, printing it and then revising on the hard copy will give you more objectivity than correcting on screen.

Something else you can do: Record the first page on an audiocassette. Do not audition for Hollywood. Read the page in the dullest monotone you can manage. If you are irreversibly histrionic, get a friend to record your page in a monotone. Don't let him rehearse, insist that he read it into the microphone before he studies it. If he hems and haws or hesitates, that's all to the good. The worse the reading, the greater the advantage to you as a rewriter. It's a good idea to avoid listening to him making the recording. Set him up and leave the room long enough for him to finish. Thank him. If he says, "Don't you want to listen?" your answer is "Later." If he insists you check that the machine actually recorded, listen to a sentence, and don't let your expression indicate anything but happiness. You'll want to let time pass and your friend or relative go home before you listen to the recording, because you want to listen very carefully not to the delivery or pronunciation but to the words.

The problem with having a friend record a page or two is that the friend is likely to double-cross you by asking sweetly afterward, could he read the whole chapter or, God forbid, the rest of the manuscript. Watch out! This is extremely dangerous. Friends and family are the least objective people in the world for manuscript-reading purposes. They like you. They might even love you. They are so pleased to see your words on paper, they will exult, they will praise, and they will mislead because your prospective readers out there are not yet your friends and will be judging your material by the emotional charge they get out of reading it. Your friends, on the other hand, will be getting their emotional charge out of knowing you wrote it.

If reading by a friend or family member is an inevitability, you can effect damage control by instructing them as follows. Ask them to put a check mark next to things they like, and a double check mark next to things they like especially. You can learn something by knowing what they approve of most, though it doesn't necessarily mean that's where you've done your best. Ask them also to put a cross next to any passage that bothers them, and an "XX" next to the worst thing they find. This limits the damage they can cause. It will also avoid the unhelpful response "I liked it" or "I didn't like it." When applied to a manuscript as a whole, or even a chapter or passage, such a response can be destructive. Remember that a friendly reader can usually tell you when something is wrong (it sags here), but comments as to how to fix it are frequently not helpful. You'll have to solve that yourself unless your relative or friend is an experienced editor. My comments are not mandated by some editors' union, they speak to the point that the editing of fiction is a high craft that takes years to learn, and you can't expect friends and relatives close at hand to substitute their intuitive reactions for experience.

Of course, if you have no friends you'd trust to tape-record your page, or don't have one handy and are in a hurry, read the page into the cassette recorder yourself, but remember that the words have to carry the meaning and stir emotion on their own. When you finish, take a deep breath and go for a long walk. If you live in Minneapolis and it's just been snowing for two days, do whatever you normally do for indoor exercise. Wash dishes. Refinish a table with water spots. Then, when some time has passed, listen carefully to the cassette on which you have recorded your page. Changing from eye to ear will give you some distance. In all likelihood, you will have an oh-my-God reaction to hearing your page, because first drafts are replete with clumsiness, inaccurate images, too many words, and imprecise renderings of what you intended to do. Not to worry. The writer's job is revision.

One mistake the majority of writers make is to revise their manuscripts starting on page one and continuing through the end. This is inefficient because the writer is fixing problems that may require changes earlier in the manuscript, involving backtracking. More important, reading a manuscript from front to back turns the writer "cold" on the manuscript, less able to judge well on repeated rereadings. To avoid these problems I developed a method of revision called Triage, after the procedure for treating battlefield casualties. In revising manuscripts, priority is given to fixing important problems first. A complete description of the process of triage for manuscripts and the steps I recommend are included in Chapter Thirty-two of *Stein on Writing*. I commend it to the reader of this book.

The big danger in revising any draft is that you will disimprove it, which is why I suggest looking at any revision of consequence carefully before implementing it. Disimprovement is much more dangerous in plays and screenplays than in novels, because the novelist has a chance to correct a serious error in galley proofs. However, I advise against waiting for galleys if possible because the author will be charged for corrections above a minimum amount, and more important, the unrevised galleys are sent out to the major early reviewers in the form of bound galleys. Authors can be damned in a review for errors that were caught at galley-correcting time, but the corrections were not seen by the reviewer. It's true that publishers put a cautionary note on uncorrected galleys, but the fact is that many reviewers don't check a final version; they've got too much to do and are frequently working against a deadline.

Disimprovement for the novelist can also be a consequence of bad advice received, usually from amateurs like family and friends. Others with authoritative personalities can provide bad advice when some authors might be vulnerable. For instance, I happened to be thousands of miles from my home base when I received galleys of *The Best Revenge* and saw to my dismay that my editor had set fourteen sections of the book in italics without asking me. Long sections of italics are very difficult to read, and are inappropriate for most novels. Resetting all those sections would be expensive, and would delay the publishing schedule. Fortunately, the president of the publishing firm was an old friend of mine, and a call to him got the matter rectified before it could do harm. Most authors won't have that advantage, but a good agent can step in when a crisis like that needs to be resolved.

I remember two instances when I was not so lucky, and I include them here because they are good illustrations of how destructive a disimprovement of written work can be. At the time I was writing plays rather than novels, and living through the excitement of a production that was in rehearsal and soon to be on its way to out-of-town showings prior to Broadway.

Playwrights have an advantage over novelists. After an initial period, live audiences witness the play on its feet. But that can also be a time of danger. The effectiveness and success of the playwright's work is dependent on directors, actors, stagehands, set designers, investors, and miscellaneous rehearsal hangers-on who can influence a production badly by making the wrong comment when everyone else is nervous and vulnerable.

The play was *A Shadow of My Enemy*, about the Hiss-Chambers case, originally commissioned by the Theater Guild and put on by a trio of well-known and excellent producers, Roger Stevens, Alfred deLiagre, and Hume Cronyn. Paul Muni was up for the lead, but he had a serious eye problem, and Ed Begley, who famously switched roles with him in *Inherit the Wind*, took Paul Muni's place. Begley was unfamiliar with one word in an important speech: "Katmandu," which is the capital of Nepal. The director explained what Katmandu is, but every time Begley came to the word, he broke into a jig and sang, "Oh the cat woman can't but the cat man do." He couldn't say the unfamiliar word with a straight face. At one point in rehearsal, Donald Oenslager, one of the great set designers of the American theater, who designed the ANTA Theater (American National Theater and Academy) as well as the play that was to have its Broadway debut there, sidled into the seat next to me. "Be careful," he whispered. "The next thing you know that speech will go. It's one of the best in the play."

Contractually, according to the Dramatists Guild, the author has the last say. But how do you deal with a star who breaks up when he comes to an unfamiliar word? You don't. The speech went. And worse disimprovement was to come.

At one of the pre-out-of-town rehearsals, a group from the New Dramatists, a wonderful organization of upcoming playwrights, was invited to watch. After the rehearsal one of the playwrights, who had a great gift of persuasion but to my knowledge has never written a successful play, proclaimed that my play, a why-done-it, should be turned into a who-done-it. This was a startling idea that called for a major rewrite while the play was in rehearsal. He convinced others. I was too inexperienced to fight back hard. I quickly had to make drastic changes in the scenes and the order of scenes, and the actors had to learn their new parts while giving eight performances a week. We all realized the change was a big mistake. The poor actors had to relearn the original version, which was hell in the middle of performances. The play moved to the National Theater in Washington, the opening attended by four justices of the Supreme Court, and then to Broadway. Serious critics like Richard Rovere and Eric Bentley praised the play, but it did not survive long on Broadway. That initial bad advice violated what today is a standard for me: *Whatever you change, don't disimprove.* That's like the warning to doctors from Hippocrates: *Do no harm.*

The day I completed this chapter I went off to New York City for a memorable reunion of the Broadway and off-Broadway playwrights of the last fifty years, sponsored by the same New Dramatists. It was a great reunion of writers, some of whose plays you have undoubtedly seen, or read, or heard about, like Robert Anderson, author of *Tea and Sympathy*, and Joe Masteroff, who wrote the book of the hit revival of *Cabaret.* The author of the bad advice for *A Shadow of My Enemy* was there, more than four decades older. He spotted me, and I spotted him. We came closer. I could read his thoughts. In all likelihood, he could read mine. We weren't wearing six-shooters. The passage of time diminishes the ire of Young Turks. He was still sticking to his misbegotten advice to change a why-done-it into a who-done-it. Fortunately, I now have a useful deaf ear.

I recall one instance of disimprovement in Hollywood, where a bestseller I had edited was being filmed and, at the invitation of the director, I was high up on an aerial perch with the cameraman, who took a marvelous shot of a car and truck crash by zooming in close to the car's left front wheel. Watching that wheel of steel bend like a doughnut was more moving than watching a car-truck crash from a distance, but the director was immediately surrounded by studio people saying, in effect, we can't spend this much money on a car crash and focus in on a single wheel! Surrounded by people from the front office demanding their money's worth, the director, an Academy award-winner, gave up, and a more conventional crash was used, which was a lot less moving than the cinematographer's shot.

Theater and film are communal enterprises, and the writer has minimal control of how the production is prepared. Novelists don't hazard the vocabulary of actors. Writing fiction is largely a solo enterprise, with all the advantages and responsibilities. With the advice of an editor, the writer has to bring a work to perfection on his own. If the writer accepts what he has written because he has written it, he is in danger. He must view the manuscript as a critic, editor, and perhaps even as a hostile exam-giver determined to find fault and to see it corrected. The writer, with his other *persona*, needs to defend his manuscript with the injunction *Do no harm*. And this process should take place before an agent or editor first sees his book.

FOURTEEN

Some Fundamentals for Emigrants from Nonfiction

All fiction writers are emigrants from nonfiction. Our past habits can be a source of trouble.

At minimum, we all write notes and letters before we turn to fiction. Our earliest mind-set is to use writing to convey information. In writing fiction our aim is to evoke emotion in the reader. The conversion can be a wrenching processs.

Vocations are seeded with handicaps for the writer new to fiction. Would-be novelists who are doctors, lawyers, academics, scientists, and other professionals have to overcome the use of jargon, words that are ostensibly designed for precision but are often used to obscure meaning from the uninitiated. In fiction, clarity is a constant. The reader who stops to puzzle out meaning has been momentarily dropped out of his experience. Members of the clergy are often dependent on audience responses based on long-held beliefs. Fiction depends on freshness. "Novel" means new. The novelist creates the world in which the reader will live for the course of the work. That is a different enterprise than the masters of other professions are used to, where, for one thing, boredom in communication is often tolerated. In fiction, it is the great sin.

Journalists and other nonfiction writers face a different obstacle. If they are reporters, of necessity they are in the habit of writing quickly, and sometimes do not see what is added or subtracted by editors before their work sees print. When they come to writing fiction, they are first draftsmen in a field in which first drafts are merely the beginning of a long process of creation, re-creation, and revision before an editor will agree to provide comment. If they are experienced in the relatively new genre of literary journalism, they are still wedded to a world of fact and truthfulness. As fiction writers, what they create—if it is good enough—becomes the truth for others.

Fiction is not a trade one plunges into, prepared to swim to success. There's not only a complex craft to learn, but a mind-set geared to creating an experience for others. Fortunately, craft can be learned. The following summary may help the writer new to fiction or migrating from nonfiction. There are eleven matters to think about before beginning to write, twenty-three to refer to while writing, six ways to get unstuck, and twenty-two matters to think about while revising.

Before Beginning to Write

1. What does your protagonist want badly?
2. Is it a desire that readers will be able to understand or identify with?
3. Who or what is in your protagonist's way? ("Who" will be more dramatic.)
4. Write a character sketch of each of the main players that has much more detail than you are likely to use.
5. Get into the skin of characters who are different from you.
6. Why would you want to spend a lot of time in the company of the person you are choosing as your protagonist?
7. How do your characters view each other? Write a short

paragraph about each character's view of the virtues, faults, and follies of the other important characters. Save these paragraphs for referral and guidance.

8. Which character's point of view will dominate?
9. How are you planning to hook the reader's attention on page one?
10. Consider starting with a scene that is already underway.
11. What are the dramatic conflicts you intend to let the reader see in each chapter?

Keep in Mind While Writing

1. The "engine" of your story needs to be turned on as close to the beginning as possible. The "engine" is the point at which a story involves the reader, the place at which the reader can't stop reading.
2. Keep the action visible on stage as much as you can.
3. Don't mark time; move the story relentlessly.
4. Is your hero or heroine actively doing something rather than being done to?
5. Substitute concrete detail for abstractions and generalizations.
6. Use surprise (such as an unexpected obstacle) to create suspense.
7. In dialogue, change perfectly formed sentences.
8. Break up long speeches.
9. Make exchanges of dialogue provocative, argumentative, combative.
10. Characterize through speech. Give different characters different speech patterns.
11. Have something visual on every page.
12. Don't tell us how your characters feel. Let the reader draw his conclusions from what each character says or does.

13. Don't resolve problems too quickly. It kills suspense.
14. Are you working on the emotions of the reader?
15. Are the obstacles facing the protagonist getting tougher as the story progresses?
16. Have you put your characters under stress?
17. Is their dialogue more revealing under stress?
18. Are you sticking to a consistent point of view?
19. Avoid summarizing unless absolutely necessary. Keep summaries very short.
20. Use sound, smell, and touch as well as sight.
21. During your descriptions of places, do you also move the story along?
22. End scenes and chapters with thrusters that make the reader curious about what happens next.
23. To increase the reader's interest, deprive him of something he wants to know.

If You Get Stuck

1. Open your dictionary at random. Dwell on each word on the page until your imagination stirs.
2. Go over the checklist above point by point, slowly.
3. Have your next paragraph reveal an unexpected turn of events.
4. Open a novel you've read and liked a lot to any page except the first and start reading slowly.
5. Interrupt the scene you're writing with an absurd turn of events.
6. Free-associate, starting with the last noun you wrote, and write down every word that comes to mind until your engine starts again.

Revising Drafts

1. Fix major problems first.
2. Cut flab, echoes, and nonessential adjectives and adverbs.
3. Check whether you have given your protagonist a flaw, a vulnerability.
4. Have you made your villain charming, interesting, strong?
5. If someone told you what your characters are doing, would you find those actions credible?
6. Is each character's motivation credible?
7. Are your characters revealing themselves, or are you doing it for them?
8. Cut down or break up any speech that runs longer than three sentences.
9. If your characters usually speak in complete sentences, revise.
10. Are responses in dialogue oblique rather than direct?
11. Have you used "he said" and "she said" instead of substitutes that describe how the words are said? Let the words and word order tell us how they were said.
12. Is there any dialogue you can make more confrontational or adversarial?
13. Delete flab to increase pace and tension.
14. Cut or cut down the narrative between scenes.
15. Have you made every word count?
16. Test every use of "very" to see if the adjective or adverb is strengthened if "very" is cut.
17. If you've said something twice in different ways, pick the better one and cut the other.
18. Are there any images or sentences you really love that don't belong in this work? Kill them.
19. If you've repeated the same noun or adjective more than once on the same page, go for your thesaurus.

20. Have you been ruthless in your cliche hunt?
21. Might your story end differently?
22. Have you been careful to avoid disimproving anything? If in doubt, leave it alone.

For the convenience of writers, the above refreshers are available on a four-sided card that can be kept next to the computer for reference. The help section in the back of this book provides a number to call for a complimentary copy of the pointers in card format.

The following questions are from relative newcomers to fiction.

1. Everybody tells me that I need to grab the reader's attention on page one. How do I do it without first describing the setting and what the character looks like?

   Show the character in action, preferably doing something that is important to the character. In the course of doing that—without stopping the story—give the reader quick glimpses of the most striking aspect of the setting *as you show the action.* For the character's physical appearance, single out an attribute that is not conventional, that conveys something about the person in a writerly way. For instance, "Carole's stammer didn't detract from her elegance." Or, "George came through the door like a truck ready to run you over." Leave room for the reader's imagination. You can use another characteristic later on in the action, but never stop the story to provide a laundry list of clothing items worn or use cliched characteristics like broad shoulders. Try to use characteristics that relate to your story, as in "he dealt with his friends as if they were employees" or "as he moved slowly across the room, age and arthritis made him seem brittle, but when he spoke—anywhere about anything—people stopped to listen as if Moses had come down with new commandments."

2. How can I create surprises readers like?

   Think of the likely logical result of what the reader is witnessing, *and have the opposite happen!* Be sure the surprise is credible and motivated.

3. My dialogue sounds stilted at times. What can I do to liven it up?

   Don't use complete sentences, don't let most characters sound logical, keep it to no more than three sentences at a time. Dialogue is an exchange. Adversarial dialogue is best. Dialogue is a new language, and takes as long to learn. The place to start is Chapter Seven. Then check the dialogue section in the "Where Writers Get Help" chapter at the end of this book.

4. What constitutes a chapter in a novel? How can I know when I've come to what should be the end of a chapter?

   A chapter consists of one or more scenes, and preferably little else. Always end your chapter with something that raises the reader's curiosity as to what will happen next, and that thrusts him into the next chapter. As to the beginning of the next chapter, *never take the reader where the reader wants to go.*

5. Someone whose opinion of my writing I trust keeps saying that my leading character seems ordinary. How can I make her more interesting?

   Give her an unusual characteristic, preferably one that relates to the story. Give her a strong want. She runs to the mailbox every day. What she's expecting hasn't come yet. You'd notice her in a pack of people because of the special way she does her hair, or the way she dresses. Imagine which of her characteristics would make you want to go off on a two-week vacation with her.

6. The novels I like best keep me turning the pages, but when I read my own stuff, after a while it doesn't keep me turning pages. Is that because I wrote it? If not, how can I put a page-turning quality into my writing?

   Keep raising the reader's curiosity and not gratifying it right away.

7. I'm told that there are parts of my plot that don't seem credible. It seems okay to me, so how do I fix it?

   Writers usually are not good judges of what does or does not come across as credible in their own work. Examine the actions that raise questions as to their credibility. Is that something you would do? Under what circumstances? Is the person doing the action sufficiently motivated? Is there a hyperbolic or cartoonish quality to the action that was questioned? Make it realistic. One of the most successful writers I have ever edited had one character throwing another character over a railing. Want to bet? Lifting a person of 170 pounds is a wrestler's job. Eliminate or change actions that are not credible when you examine them closely. Retaining not-quite-credible actions is the sign of a hack or laziness.

8. What's the "envelope," and why do some writers think it's so important?

   When you get an envelope in the mail, the return address may give you a clue as to its contents. The envelope in fiction is like that envelope. It gives your imagination something to put particulars into. "Grandma sat staring out of the window" is visual, devoid of particulars, but from the context, the reader will imagine what she might be seeing.

9. What's wrong with using flashbacks to convey a character's background or events that happened before the story starts?

   Flashbacks require a great deal of experience to be handled unobtrusively and expertly. Most flashback material can be brought into the present. If a flashback is absolutely necessary, segue into it quickly and as unobtrusively as possible, and treat the flashback itself as if it were a scene in the present. See "Help on Flashbacks" in the "Where Writers Get Help" chapter.

10. If the story is more important than the title, why is there so much fuss about getting a good title before submitting a manuscript?

    The title is the door to your book. A good-enough title will encourage readers to pick up a book and read the flaps.

11. I keep hearing my novel needs more action. Personally, I hate action movies, car chases, stuff like that, why do I have to have more action?

    You are misinterpreting the meaning of action as it is used in fiction. An exchange of dialogue is an action. Hesitating is an action. Looking away is an action.

12. I had a teacher who kept yacking about "diction" giving quality to a story. I thought diction meant how you pronounce a word correctly. What's that got to do with writing or with quality?

    Diction as used by writers has nothing to do with pronunciation. It has everything to do with selecting the precise word or image every time. That's what gives a story quality, and a writer a reputation for it.

13. I feel caught between a rock and a hard place. I know my drafts are too wordy, but if I cut a lot of words out of my manuscript, it always makes it seem too short. What should I do?

Almost all novels by newcomers that I see in manuscript are too long *for what they do.* Editors are experienced in cutting drafts, but publishers find that process costly. And paper is the most costly ingredient in a book. Hence, these days at least, shorter is better. Many of the novels I mention in this book are shorter than average. My advice is to cut all unnecessary words, especially adjectives and adverbs, and you'll see the pace of your work automatically speed up. A great way to tighten a manuscript is to cut out the worst scene. That will leave you with another scene that is now the worst. Study it. That scene may be worth cutting, too. Eliminating the weakest or unnecessary scenes always strengthens a book.

FIFTEEN

A Few Guidelines for Living Forever

A writer receiving from his editor an advance copy of his about-to-be-published book for the first time may feel his heart rhythm spring like a jack-in-the box. It's a birth. The author feels the heft of the book, admires the jacket, flips through the pages as if trying to prove to himself that the object of his attentions in manuscript for years is now actually, really, triumphantly a published book.

If that author specializes in popular entertainment and has not yet established a following, he knows the overwhelming majority of his prospective audience will wait a year to buy the book in a rack-size format whose pages will yellow and disintegrate in time. But the hardcover book is now in his hands, and he will put it somewhere, perhaps away from other books, in a place where he will see it often, at least for a week or two. Books of transient fiction are like a one-night stand, sex as entertainment. If the entertainment is good, the customer will come back for more. The author may have already begun a follow-up book, possibly with the same protagonist, for what he hopes will become a dedicated following.

In this chapter, I am addressing the author of another kind of book, one that might meld with the reader's emotions, mind, and memory like intertwining strands of DNA. This author writes with the high hope that his book will involve a union with the reader that we describe to each other with the verb "love." Such a book, the author hopes, may deserve its durable hardcover binding and acid-free pages, that God and the reviewers willing, his book may enjoy a long afterlife beyond the year of its publication, that it will become a thread in the reader's memory, that with care it may descend to a later generation like any other family heirloom. *Do read this, it was a wonderful book.*

Novelist and poet Erica Jong put it this way: "As a reader, I want a book to kidnap me into its world. Its world must make my so-called real world seem flimsy. Its world must lure me to return. When I close the book, I should feel bereft." What are the characteristics of such a work of fiction?

Certain novels have persisted beyond the generation of their writing because their themes reverberate long after we have left their pages. Herman Melville's *Moby-Dick*, Arthur Koestler's *Darkness at Noon*, Graham Greene's major novels come to mind. Most great fiction has a theme that reverberates with seemingly fresh knowledge of human nature that instructs our passions. This doesn't mean the passing of messages or information. It involves creating a world the reader comes away from with insight into the ways we deal with others. That doesn't mean didactic. The insight should derive from the story, not from authorial prescription.

Captain Ahab, who lost a leg to the great white whale Moby-Dick, is in vengeful pursuit of that beast in a "quenchless feud" with what Ahab sees as consummate evil, and that leads to his own tragic destruction.

With *Darkness at Noon*, Arthur Koestler wrote one of the few important novels that deal successfully with a major event of the twentieth century, the Soviet totalitarianism that imposed itself on much of the world for seventy years. On the same theme, George Orwell's *1984* reached a much larger audience. One should not overlook the impact of the novels of the *samizdat*, notably Solzhenitsyn's *The First Circle*, passed hand to hand in typescript in the Soviet Union, and their effect on the West when published in Europe and America.

Graham Greene, concerned also about man's depravity, wrote remarkable novels seen from an eccentric Catholicism.

These novelists—there are many others—provide the reader with fresh insight *indirectly* through their strong stories. A high percentage of surviving fiction has something of consequence to say to its readers, not through didactic authorial comment, but through the action and thoughts of the characters in the story. Huckleberry Finn is a young man who lusts for freedom, and helps define it. The fault I find in many fiction manuscripts that profess a theme is the directness with which the author argues his case instead of revealing it through the actions of his characters.

Serious fiction has a better chance of surviving when it is well taught and read. The single most distinguishing mark of such writing is the resonance of its story. It seems to expose the reader to something greater than the events of the fiction. The ending of Scott Fitzgerald's *The Great Gatsby* does that. So do the novels mentioned earlier. Resonance can be achieved by a variety of techniques, which I have described on an earlier occasion (*Stein on Writing*, Chapter Thirty-one).

Fiction that has a chance of lasting usually displays a close concern with diction, the attention paid to the choice of words, probably the best identifier of quality. The invention of accurate similes and metaphors contributes to the stature of fiction; the pursuit itself is one of the joys of writing. Literary fiction thrives on *particularity*, a precisely observed detail in place of a generality.

Another attribute for survival is the reader's memory of eccentric characters whose companionship he does not willingly forego.

Writers striving to write novels that last, in addition to reading contemporary novels of quality, should continue to read or reread novels that have survived. I remind them of what Mark Twain said. "The man who does not read good books has no advantage over the man who can't read them." In the next chapter, the reader will encounter such men. The truth about how much they influence the outcome of a writer's work is terrifying.

The Responsibilities of the Publisher

SIXTEEN

The Prospect Before Us

In this book, I have been trying to serve as a conveyor of what writers have discovered about their craft that will help lead to successful publication. Writing is not an isolated craft and at best an art. It is a profession on which the multibillion-dollar publishing industry depends. Without writing, publishers have nothing to publish. Therefore I will now turn from the writer's responsibilities for perfecting his work to the responsibilities of the publisher, and explain some of the hazards of the book-publishing industry that affect both writers and publishers.

We need to face the greatest worry that writers have once their work is ready to meet its public. *Who will judge the writer's work? Who will cast the decisive opinion to accept or reject?* This judgment affects writers who have published previously as well as newcomers, and it seems to affect writers of fiction most of all.

The answer, as I said, is terrifying.

A central worry of professional writers and many who hope to be is that in the past the decision on which books to accept and which to reject were made by editors and publishers who were book people, that is, men and women steeped in the literature of both past and present, to whom reading is an act of discovery, and to whose abode books are as necessary as walls. To publish means to put out to the world. It is common knowledge that today the decision to publish, and most particularly the degree to which a book will be "put out to the world," are influenced by sales and marketing people who, judging by their priorities, are not "book people."

The people in publishing houses who are the links to authors are its editors, most of whom are still susceptible to that initial excitement of how good a book is. An experienced editor will wonder if a particular book is a good fit in the firm's list, he will consider the size of the market for that book and how that market may be reached. Salesmen and marketers, however, have a business priority: *What is selling best now?* Most of them rely not on taste developed over many years but on recent statistics. Their operating guide is *How can we get more books like the ones that sold best last year? Is this book like book X or Y or Z?*

The priorities of marketing people rest on the assumption that the readers of next year and years to come (books are sometimes chosen years in advance of their publication) will have the same preferences as the readers of recent years. In meetings with editors the marketers insist on their guidelines: *How did the last book like that do? How did the last book from that author do? What recent best-seller is it like that we can compare it to?* Ephemeral books—fictional entertainments written by authors whose previous work was on the bestseller list, diet books, psychological pap—seem to sell best in the year of publication because they are heavily promoted but vanish from readers' shopping lists in the years to come. And so ephemera beget ephemera, and books have shorter and shorter lives, coming closer to the disposable media of newspapers and magazines instead of remaining the storehouse of a nation's culture. The controlling marketers are pushing their companies slowly onto a base of sand instead of a rock-solid backlist.

They support the payment of huge advances for books of momentary value, drive their firms to acquire the works of today's celebrities, including celebrity authors, they seem not to understand that what they are producing are hardcover magazines, and that they are taking publishing further into the area of highest risk, characterized by huge numbers of returned books and large write-offs of high author advances. They are making the same mistake as the executives of large corporations in other industries who never lift their focus from the target of quarterly earnings to look at the future. By thwarting the traditional role of publishing, the marketers may also be undermining the future of publishing as a resilient business. Publishing must be able to weather both dips in the economy and changes in taste with strong backlists of books the demand for which continues for decades.

When marketing people and the volume buyers for book chains put their emphasis on the fast sell-through of relatively few titles in an industry that produces fifty thousand new titles a year, they are not only substituting data banks for memory and judgment, they are changing the most fundamental role of publishing, the passing of culture to new generations. By focusing on imitations of what sold yesterday, the marketers are transforming the reliable economic foundation of backlist sales into an imitation of the motion picture industry, with its perpetual quest for the blockbuster that will make up for the large losses of blockbusters that have failed.

Fortunately, there are countervailing forces. On those bestseller lists that guide the appetites of the marketers, there appear regularly remarkable books of history, biography, science, and fiction *that cannot be categorized as just like some other book that sold well yesterday*. The mall stores that focused mainly on bestsellers have been overtaken by successful superstores that thrive on an astonishingly wide selection of titles. The surviving independent booksellers rely on their knowledge of books and customers, not on the vagaries of bestsellerdom. Is it possible that the marketers have lost sight of what book publishing does that is different from what magazines and movies do?

It is for the enlightenment of marketers and the hope of writers that I take you back a few decades to report an experience that should give writers heart and may give marketers pause.

In my earliest years of publishing, I knew little about bestseller lists or the commerce of books. I was familiar only with what I liked to read. In my innocence, and my impulse to share what pleased me, I began to publish a series of books undirected by marketing know-how, and in a most eccentric format. What happened fortified the little knowledge I had of what contributes to a book's survival. I had not yet begun to edit other people's fiction, so the examples I offer are nonfiction, but the books speak to the principles I've just described.

Paperbacks in the 40s and early 50s were rack-size pocket books sold mainly on newsstands and in similar outlets. Transient entertainments far outnumbered books of lasting interest. However, in the 50s, a glimmer of hope for what I thought of as my kind of book shone in the halls of a commercial publishing house. Two editors with brows above the common level, Jason Epstein, then at Doubleday, and Nathan Glazer, later a distinguished professor at Harvard, were planning a series of pocket-size books of quality that would sell mainly in bookstores.

I arranged a meeting with Glazer, whom I knew, and told him of some of the books I would like to see in what became Anchor Books. I led with a proposition to rescue a near-corpse. Bertram D. Wolfe's *Three Who Made a Revolution,* which had been published unsuccessfully some years earlier by the Dial Press, sold about a thousand copies, and for all practical purposes died. Earlier, I had edited essays by Wolfe that were published in national magazines, and Wolfe's radio scripts for the Voice of America. I was anxious to see his remarkable book back in print because of my belief that if a work is good enough, failure to sell the first time around should energize the author or publisher to try a different route. Glazer said they couldn't do the Wolfe book in Anchor because it was so long it would have to appear in three pocket-size volumes, and because they would have to be reset for the smaller format they'd have to sell more than thirty-five thousand copies of each to break even. I was heartsick. Should an important book be entombed because of its length?

Within days I came up with a plan to republish serious books by photo-offsetting them from the original editions in roughly the same size as the original books, but with paper covers to keep the price down. This process brought dramatic change to the economic feasibility of republishing good books. Such books could be profitable under ten thousand copies, which made it possible to take a chance on a far larger number of deserving books. As part of the plan, I would also publish new books in hardcover and large-format paperback simultaneously, with the thought that the hardcover would produce reviews and library sales, and the paperback would appeal to students and others for whom paper covers were then the format of choice.

I had long had an instinct for bringing opponents together for a meal so they could get to know each other as individuals. At the time of the McCarthy crisis in the United States, I brought together a Republican and a Democrat, James Rorty and Moshe Decter, to coauthor a book called *McCarthy and the Communists*, which was published by the Beacon Press and had a run of thirteen weeks on *The New York Times* bestseller list. Beacon was a good place to try out my new idea.

I phoned Melvin Arnold, the director of the Beacon Press in Boston, an intellectual with a taste for controversy and experiment. In those days I kept an egg timer on my desk to monitor the length of my long-distance calls. Within three minutes, Mel Arnold said he'd fly down to New York to discuss my plan. Soon after, I was given a contract as originator and general editor of the series and within months, a nervous young man inexperienced with sales conferences faced his first audience of salesmen with his initial list of four books.

I showed the covers. I displayed a mock-up of what we first called library-size paperbacks, a quaint name that didn't last long. The salesmen laughed. They pooh-poohed the whole idea. They said the book-size paperbacks looked like European books, not American books; paperbacks were pocket books, and how the hell do you get those larger paperbacks into a pocket? Moreover, one of the books, Wolfe's *Three Who Made a Revolution*, had been a failure in hardcover, what was the point of doing it in paperback? Besides, it was a book of eight hundred pages and contained photographs. The price would have to be $2.95. Who ever heard of charging $2.95 for a paperback? (In 1999 the same book in paperback is $14.95.) At the top of the front cover, I had put a quote by Edmund Wilson, then the leading literary critic in the United States, who called *Three Who Made a Revolution* "the best book in its field in any language." I chose that quote because Edmund Wilson had written a book on that same subject, and he was, in effect, saying that Wolfe's book was better than his own.

The sales force was still not convinced. Two of the four titles on my list were books of essays that I proposed to publish in hardcover and paperback simultaneously. The word in publishing was that essays didn't sell. As I described the books on stage in front of the sales force, I waited for someone to dart out of the wings with a hook and yank me off the platform.

In those days, unlike the present, the editorial director of the firm and not the sales and marketing people had the final say on what was to be published. Melvin Arnold gave me the green light for the series. The first four books appeared in 1955. The Wolfe book, which had sold only a thousand copies previously, in the new format sold a half a million copies in five years, and was adopted in Russian Studies courses in most American colleges and universities. The first book of essays was James Baldwin's *Notes of a Native Son,* which established Baldwin's reputation with a wide audience for the first time, and in 1999 was selected by the Modern Library as one of the "100 Best Nonfiction Books of the Century." The second book of essays was Leslie Fiedler's *An End to Innocence,* which established his reputation in the book world. I ended up editing and publishing seventeen of Fiedler's books over many decades, including a revised edition of his masterwork, *Love and Death in the American Novel.* I had set a high editorial standard for what might be included in both books of essays. Young and intolerant, I refused to include anything the writers wanted to incorporate that fell below that standard. Forty-five years later, those two books of essays are still in print.

As I had not yet been hammered by considerations of the commercial marketplace, I continued to publish books at Beacon that seemed to me to be extraordinary in the execution of their insight. The only one of the original four that did not become a classic, perhaps because of its topicality, was *A Century of Total War* by Raymond Aron, a leading French intellectual, whom *The New York Times* as late as 1999 referred to as "his country's leading commentator on the beauty and fragility of liberal society."

Things went a little easier for the neophyte publisher when he presented his second list. At the second Beacon sales meeting six months later, the salesmen had stopped laughing. As a result of the success of the new kind of paperback at the Beacon Press, Melvin

Arnold was invited to do the same for the firm then known as Harper & Row (today Harper/Collins). He eventually became its president before he retired to a forest in Oregon where, when last seen there by me, in his eighties, he was still lifting weights and the spirits of others. He used to send me one copy each of these new paperbacks, the offspring of my offspring, addressed "To Grandfather," until my shelves begged off because their burden was too great.

For several decades since that time we witnessed the proliferation and high sales of trade paperbacks of quality, bought by an educated audience for whom books are important. The reader of this book may remember that the marketers were wrong then, too, and may be again. My hope is that the reader, as a writer, will take away from this chapter not only the ingredients that lead to relative longevity in books, but also a snapshot of innovative publishing that brought serious books at low prices to a large public. The success of those large-format-paperback nonfiction books led me to include a novel in the series, André Malraux's *The Conquerors*. At the end of the twentieth century, much fiction of quality appears in that larger format with better paper and covers that are sometimes works of art. What was once a scoffed-at innovation is now a major part of publishing for the serious reader.

My age increases one year every year, but my optimism is still that of the young writer-editor-publisher who turned a deaf ear to those who are unresponsive to innovation. Some time ago Calvin Trilling remarked that most new books "have a shelf-life somewhere between milk and yogurt." As I write, technology has made possible the reprinting of books on demand at reasonable prices. Books that deserve a longer life have a new medicine. Or as my young friends say, "What goes around, comes around."

SEVENTEEN

Putting Out to the World

Can you imagine any industrial company putting out hundreds of new products a year? An insane thought! Industry, by and large, thrives on selling more of existing, successful products, and market-tests new products cautiously. The book-publishing industry, to the contrary, puts out forty or fifty thousand new products every year, mostly untested except by the intuition or experience of underpaid editors, many of whom work nights and evenings reading manuscripts because there just isn't time or opportunity during the course of a normal working day. Because the diversity among books is great, the originating publisher relies on subjective savvy more than market experience, which has far too little predictive value. Almost every book is to some extent a new product, and a season's list of those books is a business risk unmatched in other industries. Most of the authors of those books are also in a high-risk enterprise, risking years of productive time preparing an untested new product.

In this strange environment, an even stranger enmity rages. Ask any ten authors their opinion of publishers, and from nine you'll get something akin to what Mark Twain said of a publisher who had been safely dead for a quarter of a century: "My bitterness against him has faded away and disappeared. I feel only compassion for him and if I could send him a fan I would." In that old battleground between author and publisher, I am caught in the middle. I've been a writer all of my life, and a publisher of other people's books for more than half of that time. As a would-be peacemaker between the parties, I sometimes feel as helpless as a United Nations emissary trying to get Bosnian Serbs and Muslims to live in peace with each other. If I tell each side what the other side does, and some of the things they would prefer to keep secret, I find myself in no-man's-land.

As a publisher, my view was that while my company published about one hundred books a year, each author had only one book on that list, and my responsibility was to see that the prospective audience for his book knew that it was available. That was the aim. I also kept books in print far longer than I should have for economic reasons.

It was the practice of most bookshops, especially those that were part of chains, to return unsold inventory of new books after a few months, sometimes sooner. Carrying an inventory of books that sells slowly is costly to the publisher, but ever the optimist I hoped for change, which meant taking—or creating—an opportunity to repromote a book. For example, I published a book called *Deafness*, by David Wright, not a "how to" but rather a book about the experience of being deaf that I thought could be helpful to friends and family of a partially or totally deaf person. The book did not sell well for six years, but I balked at remaindering it for salvage value. If I did, it would become inaccessible to the friends and families of deaf people, of whom there were tens of millions. Perhaps I was influenced by the fact that I am deaf in my left ear and knew how much the book was needed.

Some news is good. In the book's seventh year, a doctor decided to write his syndicated medical column about that book. When the column came out, I recall we had seven thousand copies in stock and they sold out almost immediately. The author's agent knew that the cost of carrying those books for more than a half-dozen years outweighed anything we might gain from their sale. He called to thank me for hanging in there so long. Would a chief executive today insist on retaining the inventory of a book that wasn't selling for six years? With the frequent changes in the management of the firms with marketing clout, and everyone under pressure to favor the bottom line as a first priority, each book becomes an infant that has to make it in the first months of life or not at all.

My role as mediator between authors and publishers is compromised by a third occupation. I've been a working editor most of my adult life. While editors work for publishing companies, authors can develop emotional bonds with their editors that are so close, they put the married authors in jeopardy of bigamy. Many writers live inside their work, as it were. Their guide through that life, if they are lucky, can be an understanding, demanding, handholding, goading, and tough guide called an editor, who is the author's link to the good news and the bad as long as the book is in print. As an author, my closest bond was with Tony Godwin, a transplanted Englishman who became copublisher and editor at Harcourt Brace in America. Tony was venerated by his authors. Though he was a tiny man, he was a giant figure in my life. He had absolutely no right to die suddenly at the age of fifty-six, leaving me in mourning as deep as I felt on the too-early death of both my parents. As an editor, Tony Godwin was invaluable to me in my life's main work, and goaded me into writing what turned out to be my best and most successful book.

In Roman mythology, Janus was the god of gates, with two faces looking in opposite directions. As a writer, editor, and publisher, I have one more face than Janus. Can I help bring the embattled participants in publishing to an understanding of their respective roles and their interdependence? Can authors, who live on the dope of hope about their work, take the truth about the publishing process? Can the publishers of today who are mainly businessmen rather than book people understand the consequences of what they feel compelled to do for their firms' owners?

First, for the writer in the new publishing climate, a warning. If you have not yet published, you may have a touch of what I think of as the surrender disease. I see its symptoms frequently. Its victims are so eager to be published that they don't care about the size of the advance offered. If truth be known, they'd let the publisher publish without an advance, they'd even slip the publisher some money to do the deed. With any trace of that disease, the writer is sacrificing his most important card in the game, the size of the advance against royalties he is to receive. The size of that advance is what will govern a book's place on the publisher's list, the effort put behind getting copies into the stores, the effort spent publicizing the book, and much else. The publisher will lie to you about that. He will say the size of the advance doesn't matter, that they will push your book the same with a small advance as a larger advance. Don't believe it.

The publisher's effort is directed to earning back the advance through the sale of copies and subsidiary rights to third parties. If any part of the advance is not earned back through sales and licenses, the unearned part comes down as a loss to the bottom line. Therefore, the higher the advance, the harder the publisher will work to earn back the sum he guaranteed to the author. The alternative is to take sad solace in the advice one hears once in a while, "Don't throw good money after bad."

To be fair to publishers, the advance is a guarantee on a one-way street. No less will be paid even if few copies sell. If more copies or rights are sold than the publisher had estimated, the writer will receive additional income above the advance. In other words, the publisher's risk is in any part of the advance that is unearned. The publisher is also taking a risk with inventory. Don't be fooled by the relatively new capability of printing books to order, one, or fifty, or a hundred. To manufacture books at a price that will enable the book to sell in the marketplace, the publisher has to print thousands at a time. Moreover, he has to print them before he knows how well a book will do because he has to have the stock in stores before the reviews come out or the word of mouth of readers starts.

Getting every book into every bookstore is an impossible job. Bookstore owners or their buyers don't have the time to read advance copies of all forthcoming books, so they determine what quantities they will take by the size of the publisher's printing, the reputation of the author, the topicality of the book, and so on. Publishers usually exaggerate the number of copies they say they will print. If publishers had to swear under oath as to the number of copies printed of every book on a given list, they'd all get impeached. Some of the biggest business mistakes in publishing are the number of copies manufactured in a first printing. The one-time "plant" cost (typesetting and platemaking, for instance) is factored into the unit price per book on the first printing, or should be, because the publisher just can't tell whether there will be subsequent printings. Plant costs drive up the unit price, but larger printings reduce the cost per copy. The publisher is torn. The larger the printing, the lower the unit cost and the greater the margin per book. But the risk and loss increase if the books that are printed don't sell. Unsold copies end up coming back to the publisher, who will get their salvage value by selling them to a remainder dealer, usually at a loss. (The remainder dealer buys the book on a nonreturnable basis.) The more the publisher prints, the greater the chance of some books being sold at a loss. Even bestsellers, when sales drop after the umpteenth printing, have their leftover stock sold off to remainder dealers.

One major influence on the size of a first printing is whether the book will be taken at all or in quantity by the major bookstore chains. Those chains have buyers for each segment of the book market, hardcover fiction, trade paperback fiction, mass market fiction. Nonfiction buyers specialize in segments of that market, biography, history, economics, business, and so forth, with one buyer usually handling several categories or subcategories. Those hassled buyers, often underpaid for the knowledge that is required in their position, ease their hard decisions by taking cookie-cutter approaches: How many copies were sold in the chain of that author's two previous books, how many copies were sold of a similar book by someone else, how much money does the publisher say he is putting into promotion of the title, and what percentage of that is to be believed?

How can the publisher minimize his risk? He can give the writer a low advance, print a smaller number of copies. The size of the advance is what drives up both risk elements. There's no point in paying a large advance and then printing a limited number of copies.

Moreover, the publisher can't provide the same push for every book on the list, which is why the next chapter reveals why the fate of a book is usually determined before the first review comes out.

EIGHTEEN

Midlist, and Other Fictions of Publishing

Imagine a tall apartment building, ten stories high, with a penthouse on the top floor, a street-level floor, and *nothing in between.* It's impossible, the penthouse would fall down. The same is true of any publishing list. If at the top it has one or more bestselling authors, and at the bottom of the list are books that are likely to sell to libraries and not much more, that list is economically unsupportable in any publishing enterprise. Adequate publishing functions cannot be maintained only for the benefit of one or more bestsellers. Moreover, if a prospective bestseller flops, the loss can be enormous in unearned advances and remaindered books. There has to be a *list* of fifty or a hundred or two hundred or more books each season, depending on the size of the house and the amount of its fixed overhead. Yet the most dreaded, dismissive, punishing word in the publishing lexicon today is "midlist," despite the fact that the majority of books on every publisher's list fall between the very top of the list and the very bottom. That's the disgraced midlist, which every publisher has.

The term "midlist," which is applied to authors as well as books, as in "midlist authors," plagues the industry and the majority of authors on whom the business depends. The term is an outgrowth of the conversion of publishing in the last decades of the twentieth century from firms usually headed by book people to firms usually headed by people to whom books are products that bear no relation to what is passed on from generation to generation as a part of a country's culture. I have not yet seen "midlist" in any dictionary, but the term is used daily to dismiss authors and books from consideration even though every rational dismisser knows that a midlist not only has to exist, but that the majority of books on any list are midlist.

Authors live on hope. Those that live on unrealistic hope often turn their disappointment in on themselves when a book doesn't do well in the marketplace. The self is the wrong target. In the majority of instances the fate of a book has already been determined by the publisher before the appearance of the first review. Let's take a hard look at the process.

The first people to be sold the new book are the publisher's own salespersons, the ones who call on bookstores in their respective territories around the country. A national sales meeting takes place two or three times a year, depending on whether the publisher divides the year into two or three seasons. The meeting takes place several months before the season starts. At the sales meeting, the reps will hear each editor present the books the editor is responsible for.

The book or books presented by the editors with the most clout (because of their track records or positions with the house) get a lot of attention. The sales people constitute an audience, and every audience responds to some degree to presentation, the skill or enthusiasm with which a forthcoming book is announced. What counts most of all is the ranking of the books on the list, which is decided on before the sales meeting. Sometimes the ranking is a given. If the firm has paid a small fortune as an advance for a title, the book automatically moves high up on the list of its publishing season. A book by an established, well-known author whose previous books have been bestsellers will be high on the list, as will books by personalities celebrated in other fields who have easy access to the media. A book can move up the list because other people with money to offer like it; that is, if the two major book clubs have competed for it or paperback rights have drawn a big advance, or movie or foreign rights have been sold for large sums prior to the meeting.

Once upon a time a major prepublication license to a paperback house could result in a book being positioned higher up on the list, often because the licensee required a big advertising budget as part of the deal. Paperback editors competed aggressively to buy the titles that were already high on the publisher's list, eager to pay too much money in order to keep a title out of the hands of their competitors. With almost all of the major publishers now owning their own paperback companies, the big paperback sale to another publisher is much less frequent, and therefore less likely to affect the book's position on the publisher's list.

The position of all books on a publisher's list is determined by a group that will usually include the director of marketing, the sales manager, the head of publicity and promotion, perhaps the editor-in-chief, perhaps the publisher. In most houses, it is the marketing and sales directors, not the editors, who have the greatest influence on the order of the books on the list. An inexperienced author eavesdropping on this meeting might conclude that these friendly people were actually deciding which books will live and which will die, or at least which will sell a lot of copies without doubt, and which, at the bottom of the list, will be sent to market without publicity, promotion, advertising, or anything else that will tell the public that this baby is born and wishes its unique cry to be heard.

It wasn't always this way. Some decades ago, if an editor truly loved a book and gave his heart to its presentation, it would have some effect on the rest of the publishing team. As publishing became a bottom-line business, love was replaced by money; what counted was the amount guaranteed to the author that had to be earned back from sales of the book. That is now the driving force that garners advertising and promotion money for a book and thrusts it up the list.

At the sales meeting, each of the books at the top of that season's list is announced with fanfare. The assembled force will hear the quantity of the first printing, important evidence to them and to their bookstore customers of the publisher's commitment to the book and expectation for its early sales. Time will be devoted to the promotion plans. An advertising schedule and sample ads will be distributed with sales kits. If the author is to be sent on tour, a list of cities with tentative dates will be distributed. Advance quotes from successful authors may have been collected. The publisher may have prepared bound galleys that look like hardcover-size paperbacks, a special edition for advance reading that doesn't have to be read; the fact that it has been printed and distributed to the trade is enough to convince booksellers that this book will be pushed by the house. An exceptional novel will sometimes capture the attention of booksellers by means of bound galleys. The bookseller has grown accustomed to asking, "What else are you doing for the book?" and being guided by the answer in deciding whether or not to stock enough copies for face-out display in the store.

At the sales conference, as the editors take turns and move down the list, the sales people will hear the title, author, an alleged printing size, price, and the handle, which is a short description of the book designed to evoke interest in it. The editor may mention that the author will give readings in his local area, or do a newspaper interview. This washes over the audience because it means there is no national campaign to attract readers in every salesman's territory.

Are there exceptions? Of course. If Oprah Winfrey selects a book, that's a signal to the publisher to print a million copies and go all out in promoting it. An occasional sleeper or a book of particular quality will intrigue an influential reviewer, who will give it undreamed-of space. Sometimes a book is "hand-sold" by independent booksellers who are in love with it and recommend it to customers, though these rarely sell in large quantities. Sometimes a book of zero literary merit will sell because the author is willing to travel by car to every town in America that has a paucity of local authors but has a bookstore whose owner—or an influential clerk—can be charmed. Jacqueline Suzanne started it in the 60s with *Valley of the Dolls* and Robert James Waller continued it in the 90s with *The Bridges of Madison County.*

Flukes will happen. A military book about a World War II campaign advanced more than any other title in Texas, and didn't do particularly well elsewhere in the country. On investigation, it turned out that the salesman in Texas had been in that campaign and had a once-in-a-lifetime chance to tell his war stories on the road.

Fine novels and deserving nonfiction also sometimes get a lucky break, and literature survives.

The publisher's salespersons take orders from booksellers months before the physical copies are available. The sales rep presenting many dozens of new books may have had an opportunity to read only the books deemed by the publisher to be lead books. For the rest, the salesman has to rely for his pitch on the catalogue copy or what the editor of the book said at a sales conference. The salesman has about thirty seconds to convey the title, author, price, size of printing, and what the book is about. In most circumstances the handle can only be a sentence or two. If the book is by an author with a track record, the buyer is reminded of it.

Obviously the rep presenting fifty or a hundred or two hundred titles, having discussed the promotion plans for the lead titles, can't take the time to be fair to all the other titles on the list before the bookstore buyer, his attention span over, declares "Enough!" That means the sales reps voluntarily skip some titles altogether. The salesman in the field becomes the chief decision maker, pulling the life support off the skipped books. Those unmentioned books, usually from the bottom of the season's list, will never be sold in that bookstore unless something miraculous happens somewhere else and the bookstore hears about it.

Most bookstore and chain buyers will order titles in proportion to their positioning on the publisher's list. In the smallest stores, only the top books may be bought, or books on subject matters that have a following among the customers of that store. In larger stores that can and do represent most of a list, the books that are bought in the largest quantity will be shown face out. The books that are bought in ones and twos will be spine out, which reduces their chances of being seen by the browser. Books bought in small quantities for spine-out display usually experience a high return rate. So do books by bestselling authors that are oversold because of past accomplishment or imaginative expectation. Shopping mall bookstores, now on the wane, introduced book buying to many people who were intimidated by bookstores and afraid that if a clerk asked them what they wanted, they'd be paralyzed for an answer. But these mall stores could sell in quantity only the "big" books, displayed in dumps up front or on the narrow ends of display islands, called end caps, which, in case you didn't know it, are rented by the publisher, and therefore available only for titles high up on the list that have a budget for in-store promotion.

Display space is not the only thing rented. The books themselves are really rented rather than bought by the bookstore because they can be returned, usually any time up to one year from the time of purchase. So when a publisher or editor represents that a book has "sold" ten thousand copies, it means that ten thousand copies have been placed in stores on the equivalent of consignment, subject to return. And the hard fact is that about 40 percent of new books—especially novels—are usually returned and remaindered, meaning sold for salvage value, with no royalty to the author.

The size of the first printing as announced to or by the sales reps or in print to the trade is often greatly exaggerated by certain firms. The bookstore buyer isn't always fooled. The largest exaggerations are for the "biggest" books.

The same is true for the size of the advertising or marketing budget. The books that will sell best are almost always the books that the publisher pushes or promotes the most, a decision you now know was made prior to publication. The absence of advertising for any book is a pain in the author's pride more than a detriment to sales. Few books sell as a result of space advertising. The key activities for selling books are *publicity* and *visibility* where books are sold.

Can any outside influence affect the positioning of a book? Yes. Licenses to major book clubs are almost always arranged at least four months prior to publication. A main selection at the Book-of-the-Month Club or the Literary Guild can influence the positioning of a book somewhat. That happens to several dozen books a year, most of which have already been positioned high on the publisher's list, which may be one reason the book clubs picked them. After all, books heavily promoted by the publisher have a better chance of selling to book club members. Selection as an alternate of a major club or by one of the one hundred or more clubs that are smaller than the Literary Guild or Book-of-the-Month Club will usually not influence a book's positioning.

Most first-time authors—and others, too—are so happy to have a publisher accept a book that they don't think much about positioning, or don't know about it, even though positioning will influence the fate of the book significantly. Is there anything an author or his agent can do to try to influence a book's place on the publisher's list? Obviously the advance obtained for the book means more than just money. If anyone working for the publishing firm says the advance does not influence positioning, they are lying. Is that commonplace? Yes. Are authors gullible in this respect? Yes. Even experienced authors? Yes. And agents? Remember that an agent has to be something of a psychotherapist. If all he can get for the author is a modest advance, he wants the author to be happy nevertheless, so he will encourage the author to believe the editor who is saying that there is more hope for the book than has already been determined by the size of the advance.

If you are promised promotion or advertising for your book, it would help if that ends up in your contract as a commitment, at least as to a minimum. Editors move around, and an absent editor's verbal promises of a year ago are written on sand in a sandstorm. Don't be surprised if even the best agents can't get a contract commitment for advertising or promotion because it is rarely forthcoming.

An agent can try to keep the paperback rights free for competitive bidding. If two paperback companies like the book well enough, competition could drive the price up. The hardcover publisher might—just might—adjust the book's position on the list.

Once upon a time most editors could be counted on to support a book they acquired through the publishing process. Editors with good in-house reputations were relied on by others in the organization. Today, the predominant influence is from the sales side of the firm. Still, some editors have a way of charming sales people into glancing at a manuscript. Some marketing directors actually read all or part of a manuscript that a reliable editor is enthusiastic about. There are still editors around who influence their houses a good deal. If your agent can get your manuscript into the hands of such an editor, your chances for good positioning are greater. The outcome often depends on which editor within the house received the manuscript. Many agents prefer to submit a book to the highest-ranking editor they know well, but books bought by the head editors are often delegated to editors lower in the pecking order who will have less influence on the publishing process. It can be said that a book's positioning is determined not only before the first review appears, but much earlier when the agent submits it for consideration. In fact, the reputation of the agent doing the submitting matters. There are reportedly nearly a thousand literary agents in North America alone, but fewer than a dozen have clout. By clout I mean the editor to whom a manuscript is directed will seize and open quickly any package arriving from that agent, who is known to have big-name or recently successful authors in his stable.

A point you don't want to lose sight of is that publicity is the most cost-effective means for letting the public know a particular book exists. Nothing prevents the author with energy and personality from stepping forward to promote his own book if the publisher is not doing enough. Whatever the publisher does, in the author's eyes it will never be enough, and the author is often right.

Envoi

NINETEEN

Welcome to the 21st Century

It's like taking a leisurely drive along a familiar road and having a truck whoosh past in the opposite direction every few minutes, a huge blur carried by a blast of wind. That's the effect technology has had on me as a writer. Chances are you're younger than I am, maybe a lot younger, so let me convey what it was like to experience rapid change.

My first writing that could be called creative were stories written in pencil. There were no ballpoint pens yet, and fountain pens were for rich people, kids didn't carry them. I penciled my primitive stories on the blank lines of yellow Western Union telegraph pads stolen by my father as he passed through Grand Central Station. We couldn't afford writing paper during the depth of the Depression. There weren't many blank lines on the short telegram blanks, so a story, however short, took a lot of blanks. I also wrote poems, which suited the short space better. When I was seven, one of the poems got published in the school paper. It scanned and made sense. The rhymes rhymed. Though I later had poems published in reputable magazines, that first one is the only one I can recite by heart. Four or five years later, when I was still a pre-teen, a new

New York newspaper conducted a verse contest as a promotion stunt. A stamp was what, three cents? I wrote a poem, and, one day, reaching for the mail, I spotted a letter from the newspaper. Were they sending my poem back? They should just have tossed it. Inside the envelope was a check for twenty-five dollars, which made me the richest kid in my neighborhood.

Kids have a frightful audacity sometimes because they don't know the adult rules. When I was twelve, I took up magic as a hobby. When I was thirteen, I mixed my lust to write and my new hobby by writing a book about it. I typed all the pages on a manual typewriter. I don't remember the typewriter, I just remember fussing with carbon paper, trying to get more than one copy by coming down hard on each key. It hurt every time I made a change because I had to retype the whole damn page, pounding to get that blue of the carbon copies readable. I sent the face copy to a New York publisher who specialized in magic books. He asked to see me. When I went, the first thing he asked me was, why didn't my father come himself. I got somebody with a name to write the introduction so people would believe I was the author. It stayed in print longer than most books do now.

I knew the Depression was coming to an end when I was given a real typewriter like grown-ups used. The carbons came out better. World War II took me away from my writing for a couple of years, but it wasn't too long before IBM invented a neat electric typewriter. By neat, I mean the appearance of the page. If you want to experience the benefits of technological change, compose a story in pencil, then type the story on a portable that shakes the glass of water on the table when you type. Finally, type a story on an IBM Selectric, especially the later model that enables you to backspace over a letter and erase it! Wow! When it became easier to fix errors, suddenly I became much less tolerant of my first-draft errors in craft and judgment.

I never did get a word-processing machine, though I did watch over my friend Renni Browne's shoulder as the machine remembered what she had written and could print it on demand. (I still don't understand why we say print it *out.* Where else could it go?) The big change in my technological advance was thrust upon me in July of 1987 when my daughter, then a student at Columbia College, now an editor of many distinguished bestsellers, dragged me to some place way out in New Jersey and forced me to buy a Kaypro computer with thirty megabytes of hard disk space, enough to hold nearly a hundred novels. This miraculous machine made revision much easier. As recently as the 1960s and 1970s and into the 80s, transpositions of clauses, sentences, and paragraphs required retyping a page. Making clean copies of new drafts of articles, stories, and book-length manuscripts was a labor-intensive task, stealing the writer's time or costing much to pass the labor on to others who typed quicker or better. At least as important is the fact that the computer preserves writing, which hasn't kept some adults from writing the same novel over and over again.

I have a lot to be grateful for in the rapid advance of technology. I created four computer programs that are used by over a hundred thousand writers in thirty-eight countries, who seem to be happy because they send grateful letters. The programs provide enough royalties for me to feed a roost of pigeons, if I kept pigeons. What I don't like is the amount of time that is demanded of me by Bill Gates and other software sponsors to learn and relearn all kinds of things that are irrelevant to my purpose, being able to type my books and make changes easily.

I am also a mite concerned about other dangers to the writer inherent in some of the changes we are facing in the new millennium. I sound like a neo-Luddite when I wax nostalgic over WordStar, a DOS program that in its ads boasted the names of writers who used it. I still use it to write all my fiction, as I ignore the laughter of my technology-dependent friends. What writers want is not a pinball machine on their screen, but the near-equivalent of a blank page. We want to spend our time writing instead of computing, with minimum interference from the technology. My car, a technical marvel that has transformed the world, works fine without my getting on a help line and having to wait a half hour until a human being answers. The computer should speed our work, not rob our time.

Once upon a time that stretched over centuries, writers wrote letters in which they worried their lives, or shared their solutions for the fate of the world with friends or lovers. When those writers died, the remains of their correspondence became the stuff of biographers, and enabled later generations to know their lives. One of the tragedies of modern life is that we don't write thoughtful, anguished, hopeful letters much anymore. We communicate by e-mail, a quick query or answer. Of course e-mail is a wonderful way of, say, asking questions of someone in a different part of the world and getting an almost immediate response. For the writer as guardian of his language, however, e-mail brings a danger into common play: an e-mail letter is usually a first draft, and you all know by now how hazardous first drafts are to writers. E-mail encourages sending thoughts off the top of the head, not carefully crafted, not nuanced, not conveying a person's voice. The great advantage of hard copy is that it gives us a different perspective on what we have said perhaps glibly, and provides a semblance of objectivity to correct errors and awkwardness. The proliferation of first-draft writing worries me, as it will worry the biographers of future generations. The habit of pushing first drafts out into cyberspace can affect a writer's work immensely: Get it out instead of get it right.

I see an additional danger in the publication of works on the Internet. The complexity and expense of publication in magazines and books require standards of acceptance. As I write, easy publication on the Internet lowers those standards precipitously. You are what you read, and if you read a lot of what's published as creative writing on the Internet, you can throw everything you may have learned in this book away. I have been alarmed about the freefall of education for half a century. I have met serious writers who are undereducated in the books that have preceded theirs.

We need to reacquaint ourselves with the writings not so much of our neophyte contemporaries but of the writers before us who mastered their craft. You don't have to scroll half-pages in a book. You can read as slowly or intensely or as rapidly as you like at any given moment. Pray let us not lose what we have gained, the main method of passing culture from one generation to the next, in order to accommodate people who are proud to call themselves nerds. Let us suck every bit of knowledge we can to fortify our power as writers, our ability to move, amuse, and inform. In the new millennium, I hope writers will be known as book people. I know no higher compliment.

Publication of a book that you can hold in your hands and read at your own pace has many advantages beyond the one that was adduced by Elia Kazan's mother when she came to see me shortly after the publication of his first book, *America America*. She said she could not show her son's plays and movies to her friends, mostly elderly Greek women like herself who did not go to the movies or frequent theaters on Broadway. With the publication of *America America*, she said, waving the book in her hand, she at long last had something to show her friends. As the editor of that now-classic book, I can tell you that it took the kind of thought and work that is bypassed in premature Internet publication. Published in the form that Kazan's mother held aloft proudly, it took four drafts after the author thought he was finished, but the published version established Kazan in the art of writing, which he ended up preferring to those of theater and film, in which he has been so much honored.

Making a movie is a communal activity. So is putting on a play. A book, even with the best of editing, is essentially the work of one person, its author, before the publisher takes it out to the world.

The computer is a tool. E-mail is a means. Writing can be an art.

Take the long view. A few centuries ago a book might circulate a few copies. The number of people who read novels in the first half of the twentieth century is tiny compared to the numbers who buy and read novels today. There has been an astounding revolution in readership. The quantities of successful books sold are staggering compared to the sales of just a few decades ago. And the number of titles of fiction of literary quality readily available in quality paperback form continues to astonish and please me, a publisher of the old school. It is sad to see so many privately owned booksellers displaced by chains, but the reality is that the better chains carry a much greater selection even of specialized books than most bookstores once could afford to. I loved some of the booksellers I got to know like family. They, like publishers of my vintage, loved not only books, but the aura of books. However, in time our air became thin, and there were no societies protecting our perhaps outmoded environment. I remember when my mother-in-law, an avid reader of good books, had to wait for a family excuse to drive hundreds of miles from her home in Iowa to Chicago to experience the joy of browsing in a really good bookstore, which her great-grandchildren today can do easily. If the grandchildren are lazy, or glued to their computers, they can browse both new and old bookshelves online.

I remember how hard it was to find out-of-print books, including my own, until I discovered bibliofind.com on the Internet, which enables me—or anyone else in the world—to browse among nine million used books and find what I want in minutes, most at a fair price. Writers all over the world are in touch with each other via the Internet. In this remarkable new world, scientists have cloned one sheep from another, and I have cloned myself. I used to talk to as many writers as could squeeze into whatever room or auditorium was made available to us. Now, through my computer programs, I whisper in the ears of writers in thirty-eight countries as they learn the craft and improve their drafts.

Crust is good on bread but not on brains. Readership and the availability of books are on the rise. Despite the conglomerating of publishing firms, more fine writing is available to more people at reasonable cost than ever before. When I realize that more than a million people bought a novel of mine called *The Magician*, I think that could never have happened in any previous century. Writing is better than any other type of work because you don't get downsized, nobody can take your license away, and you avoid all the diseases caused by boredom. Writing is the second most exciting activity a higher power invented for human beings. And when you get to your eighties, it's the first most exciting activity. With all those readers now reachable, the new millennium is an exhilarating time for writers to bring their characters to life and their insights to the world.

Practical Matters

TWENTY

Appendix One: The Little Things That Damage the Writer's Authority

Those little things are like acne to a teenager, each blemish small in size but oh how damaging the overall impression can be, especially when first seen. Elsewhere in this book I have mentioned some of the glitches that momentarily disturb the reading experience. Curing glitches is part of learning craft.

Eye-stoppers, glitches in the reader's experience, can undermine the writer's authority even in an otherwise excellent story. The writer who neglects these matters sabotages the reader's experience, which is why I deal with such glitches here.

Because readers read whole words fast, a glitch is anything that causes them to see the letters on the page. They are momentarily yanked out of their experience. Dialect, using spelling to convey a regional, ethnic, or class deviation from the norm, is a continuous glitch wherever it appears. Dialect was used for the speech of black Americans until James Baldwin used rhythm and word order to convey black speech. The eccentric spelling of dialect is useless to the people from the region where the dialect exists because they pronounce words spelled normally as if they were in dialect. Dialect spelling therefore comes across to them as a glitch. Worse, however, is the fact that the spelling of dialect always calls the reader's momentary attention to the letters on the page, breaking the experience. The writer is trying to keep that experience unbroken, recognizing that such experiences, especially if deep, are just what readers most enjoy. Dialect sabotages the writer's intent and the reader's pleasure. Not much. Just a glitch. Readers aren't aware of what's happening, but if it happens repeatedly, it affects the writer's authority.

There are other kinds of glitches that cumulatively damage the writer's authority. Dashes, indicated in manuscript by two hyphens without a space at either end, should be used rarely, and only for interjections. The most common use of dashes in fiction is to indicate that a line of dialogue is interrupted by another speaker.

It may seem as if we are about to shift to more-trivial matters, those that concern the appearance of the manuscript. Appearance is not trivial because the wrong appearance is detrimental to the reception the writer's manuscript will get when it reaches the agent or editor. The authority of the writer derives not only from the writing, but from how it is presented. An amateurish presentation will prejudice the busy agent or editor who doesn't want to deal with inexperienced amateurs.

Think of a manuscript that arrives in an editor's hands with a fanciful drawing on its top page, and bound with ribbon. (I've seen things like that in my career.) The editor's immediate reaction is "This is from an amateur," which can cause the editor to dismiss the manuscript without reading a word. Even if the editor is patient, an amateurish-appearing manuscript—the wrong typeface, single-spacing, insufficient margins—can undermine the author's authority in the eyes of the professional reader.

I must admit to being surprised whenever I find writers who dress their manuscripts the equivalent of a job interview in a bathing suit with spangles. One of my intentions throughout this book has been to provide the writer with techniques that will ease the pebbled path to publication. Therefore I can't in good conscience skip some elementary details that telegraph the wrong message to the agent or editor.

TYPEFACES. The typeface you use for your manuscript matters. The wrong typeface is more of a hazard than it used to be because of all the fancy typefaces available to the writer who works on a computer. Those fancy typefaces are for other things, not for a manuscript that wants to pass as professional. A simple reason dictates the use of Courier, a standard nonproportional typeface available in all the word-processing programs I've seen. That's what the recipients are used to from typewriter days. That's the type most professional fiction writers still use today. And it should be twelve-point type, both for easy readability and for its resemblance to the size of pica typewriter type. Some writers prefer to use Times Roman, the most common proportional typeface, in which the letters have different widths. Times Roman is an attractive typeface, and is common in business. But if it's fiction you're writing, Times Roman has a hidden hazard. There are a much greater number of words per line and page, which has the effect of making the reading experience seem slower. Pages are turned less frequently. A page using Courier seems to move much faster. That's a psychological advantage not to be slighted.

Under no circumstance use a sans serif typeface like Ariel or Helvetica for text of any length. That goes for articles as well as book-length manuscripts. The letters of a sans serif typeface are stick figures without curlicues. A serif typeface has little curlicues coming off the beginnings and ends of letters, as in the type you are reading right now. What those curlicues do is link the letters in a word. We read words, not individual letters. That's why a serif typeface is easier to read. Sans serif is okay for headlines or picture captions—short material—but anything that's a paragraph or longer should be in a serif typeface for readability. The problem, especially in business, is that designers like the looks of sans serif typefaces. (The condensed versions of sans serif typefaces enable one to squeeze more letters in per inch.) The designer is interested in the appearance of a page, not in its readability. You are interested in its readability.

I sense a slow adaptation to italicized words appearing in actual italics since that is now possible with most word processors. The standard method until the 90s was to underline the words you wanted italicized.

Avoid boldface in fiction. The words have to do the work, not the typeface. Boldface is used in this chapter, the help chapter, and the glossary for easy reference.

Line spacing. Just yesterday I was shown a manuscript by an author who has published only one book, years ago. It has become a classic, and is in its fourth edition. Now he's completed a work of fiction, and the manuscript is single-spaced. I immediately phoned him and asked why he'd done that. He said, "To save paper."

The agent or editor will not think it's a fair trade-off, his eyesight against the author's trying to save paper and postage. All manuscripts should be double-spaced, even the drafts you do for your own examination, so that you will be experiencing them the same way the professionals will see them.

When you want to indicate a change in location or the passing of time in fiction, skip four lines instead of two. We call that a "line space." You don't need to put an ornament in the blank space unless it falls at the very beginning or end of a page.

MARGINS. Some writers attempt to deceive the recipient by hving larger-than-usual margins to make a manuscript seem to have more pages, or vice versa. You're not fooling anybody, just causing inconvenience. To my knowledge, no publisher requires writers to use prescribed margins. One inch on all four sides is fine. The sides of the page should be the same. A bit more on the top of the page is okay, too.

Do not under any circumstance justify your type; that is, have the right margin aligned as in printed text. All that does is shout amateur. It will also make some of your lines look funny, with too much space between some words.

PAGINATION. Your pages must be numbered, starting with the first page of actual text, not the title page or other front matter. Where on the page to put the number? Some sources recommend the top center or the top right or the lower right. I have a sly suggestion. If your word processor permits putting the number at the bottom centered, you might consider doing that for the same reason I do: it is less intrusive in the reading process. Numbers at the top of the page tend to be noticed by a reader, even for a split second. At the bottom right numbers are sure to be noticed as one turns to the next page. I want undivided attention given to the words in the manuscript, so I put the numbers in the least obtrusive place.

RUNNING HEADS, sometimes called headers, refer to words that appear on the top of every page of a typescript, such as the title and/or author's name. I disapprove of the use of running heads because they consist of words, and the reader cannot help but see those words as he is turning pages. You don't need to remind the agent or editor reading your manuscript of your name or the title of the book. If your pages are numbered, that's sufficient to prevent a most-unlikely mix-up, particularly if you follow my advice and put the page numbers in the middle of the bottom of the page, where they are least likely to be seen as the reader turns pages. You don't want the reader to be aware of how many pages he's read. Keep the reader's mind locked into the experience.

FRONT MATTER. Don't use large or fancy type for your

title. It says "amateur." Use the same type as for your manuscript. For a book-length manuscript, you may put the approximate number of words in the upper-right-hand or lower-right-hand corner. Don't say 76,342 words, even if you've run a computer word count. A rounded number, 76,000, will do. Put your name, address, phone, and fax number, and e-mail address if you have one, in the lower-left corner of the title page. An agent will usually cover this with a sticker that has the agency name and address before it goes to the publisher.

In the case of a nonfiction book, be sure to include a table of contents. Do not prepare an index until your editor asks you to. For most books that require an index, professional indexers are available. Your word-processing program may have an indexing feature, but wait till you have a final manuscript that's been copyedited to do indexing, because the page numbers will change.

If you are going to dedicate the book to someone, put the dedication on a separate page. If you are going to acknowledge the help of people, do that in an acknowledgment, also on a separate page. I suggest that you don't include those pages in submitted manuscripts. Wait till the manuscript has been contracted for. You might just want to add the name of the editor or anyone else in the publishing house who provided significant help.

BINDING THE PAGES. Never bind the pages of fiction or nonfiction. Editors read manuscripts one page at a time. They may take a group of pages to read on the train or at home. They may want to pass the pages already read to someone else in the publishing house to see if they agree that it's a wow of a book. Always transmit the loose pages in a box in which the manuscript fits snugly. If it's not snug, put spacers in that will keep the pages from moving around. Or cut a piece of foam board, available in art supply stores, to the same size as your manuscript pages. Cut cardboard will also do as a reinforcing agent. Never use plastic peanuts to fill up a manuscript box. Peanuts generate ill will at the receiving end. Use bubble wrap in the extra space if you can't find foam board or clean cardboard. If you use a flimsy box, the kind that paper sometimes comes in, be sure to put that box into a sturdy box for shipping. There are file folders that are closed on three sides and that expand to about two inches that I've been using for manuscripts for many years. I put a label on the front. That accordion folder offers additional protection for the manuscript, and is also convenient for the editor at the receiving end, something my experience makes me think of often.

PLAYS AND SCREENPLAYS. If your manuscript is a play, it should be three-hole punched and bound in a standard colored folder that comes with three built-in brass fasteners. If you take your manuscript for reproduction to a commercial copy place, be sure to have them copy your play script or screenplay on three-hole paper. The standard folders used for plays usually have a place for a label on the front. If you use a laser printer or ink-jet printer, you can print the manuscript directly on three-hole paper, which is widely available at large stationery supply centers or by mail order.

A screenplay is bound differently. It should have a cover sheet and a back sheet on colored stock that is heavier than paper. Choose lighter colors for the cover stock so that you can print the title and your name on the front cover. You can print the screenplay on three-hole paper. Punch three holes in the front and back cover. The covers sandwich the pages of the screenplay, and are held together with round-head brass fasteners inserted through the front. If you want to appear knowledgeable in matters of movie-industry custom, use the fasteners for the top and bottom hole and leave the center hole unfastened. Don't ask me why. If you know, tell me.

There are now computer programs that will automatically do

most of the complex formatting required for plays and screenplays, and television scripts also. They enable you to concentrate on the writing instead of the formatting. The best way to learn the correct format for a screenplay is to look at a sample script. Paperback manuals for screenplay formatting are available but seeing the format and using it are separate worlds. To stay sane, you'll eventually need a screenplay formatting program that will put all the necessaries in the right place. I've recently become acquainted with one called Final Draft, that comes in both Windows and Macintosh versions and can be converted from one platform to the other readily. It has the facility to let you restructure the order of scenes, and can Undo up to twenty previous actions if mistakes are made. You can find out more about Final Draft by calling (800) 231-4055, faxing (818) 995-4422, or writing to Final Draft, Inc., 16000 Ventura Blvd. Suite 800, Encino, CA 91436.

LENGTH. How long should your book be? Long enough to do the job, which is probably shorter than its present length if you haven't revised it ruthlessly. Once upon a time, long was good. Now the price of paper is such an important consideration, you may have noticed that publishers are putting out some pretty short books. For nonfiction, the cost restriction isn't as great because the price to the consumer is more flexible. People will pay more for a nonfiction hardcover book than they will for a novel. A good length for a novel is 75,000 words, topping out perhaps at 100,000 words. Longer than that is a hazard except for bestselling authors and certain genres. If you follow my earlier suggestions, and if your manuscript is running about 300 words to the page, 250 pages will give you a 75,000-word book, give or take a bit. If your novel runs 700 pages or longer, the agent or editor on the receiving end is going to emit a loud sigh, which means that even if the novel is terrific, it's either going to involve some heavy cutting suggestions on his part or a hard sell to the economic watchdogs at the publishing house. I know, Tom Wolfe's *A Man in Full* is very long. So is his reputation. The publisher made up for the length of the book by printing more than a million copies at once, saving on the printing. Tom Wolfe and Norman Mailer are entitled to write long books if they choose to. I am addressing writers who need every advantage in getting past the publisher's door, and at the time of writing, short is good. The manuscripts I see are almost invariably too long for their stories. I told one of my students to take advantage of his computer's capabilities and cut out all of his adjectives and adverbs. The manuscript turned out to be 72 pages shorter, and, of course, the elimination of the adjectives and adverbs made it stronger.

TWENTY-ONE

Appendix Two: Where Writers Get Help

Help in Books for Writers

As an example of strong fundamental plotting, I recommend Barnaby Conrad's novel *Matador*. The Capra Press edition contains a longish afterword called "The Writing of Matador" that writers should read. Not mentioned there is the fact that *Matador* was first optioned for film by John Huston, and by others since, including one well-known Hollywoodian who suggested taking that bullfight story and converting it to boxing! That's how many members of the film community use their imaginations. Hollywood can be thought of as an island where a different language is thought and spoken, where sometimes absurd ideas are misnomered "high concepts," and where a writer's writing life has been in danger since the days when William Faulkner, Scott Fitzgerald, and Sinclair Lewis were lured there. Amazon claims *Matador* is out of print. Write to the author, Barnaby Conrad, at 8132 Puesta del Sol, Carpenteria, CA 93013. He's stashed a few copies of the Capra Press edition, and he'll sell one to you at $18.95, plus $3 postage. He won't charge for autographing it if you ask him to.

Some writers have difficulty being candid, though candor is a hallmark of some of the most successful fiction of the current period. Earlier in this book, I recommended reading *Elia Kazan: A Life*, Kazan's autobiography, one of the best of this century. I have read the book four times. Out of print in its original Knopf editions, a new paperback edition has been published by Da Capo Press and is available from bookstores or online from amazon.com or barnesandnoble.com.

Some writers like exercises with their instruction. I can recommend *Self-Editing for Fiction Writers* by Renni Browne and Dave King. Ms. Browne is the founder of the Editorial Department, the first national organization of independent editors. If she ever addresses a writers' group in your area, do listen, she's a dynamic speaker.

The Art & Craft of Novel Writing by Oakley Hall is a good elementary book on craft.

A tiny and largely unknown book of only 123 pages called *The Craft of Writing* by publisher and editor William Sloane is a favorite of mine, now easily available in a paperback edition published by Norton. The book was put together by Sloane's widow from his letters and critiques to writers. His instruction is excellent.

Writers who long to write for the movies need a guide that is both realistic and frank. A busy writer named Skip Press has taken a lot of trouble to put together a useful guide to the movie-making community. It's called *Writer's Guide to Hollywood Producers, Directors, and Screenwriter's Agents*. This large-format paperback published by Prima is not just a listing. It contains much substantive information and comment with each entry. The author's interviews with producers and others provide valuable insight into how the film world works, and where you can get some formal training.

Reference books for writers are listed in a separate category below. For answers to legal matters affecting writers, see "Help with Legal Issues."

Help with Characterization

The creation of credible, interesting characters is the fiction writer's primary obligation. Fortunately, a lot of help is now available. In addition to Chapter Five of this book, I'd like to call your attention to three chapters in *Stein on Writing*: Chapter Four of that book, "Competing with God: Making Fascinating People," is a good place to get started. The chapter that follows it, "Markers: The Key to Swift Characterization," is important for both the serious mainstream novelist and the writer of escape fiction. Chapter Twenty-nine, on particularity, will also be helpful.

In software, the choice depends on where you are in your work. WritePro® is a quasi-interactive, award-winning tutorial program that prevents writer's block as it teaches by what is acknowledged to be the best method available: you use everything you learn immediately, which helps you remember the techniques when you need them. WritePro comes in individual lessons. By the end of Lesson Two even beginners will have created a protagonist and an antagonist (hero and villain), and written one or two scenes using those characters successfully. If you already have a substantial amount of manuscript and are interested in determining any faults it might have in characterization, or if you want to enhance your existing characters, I highly favor the Characterization Module of FictionMaster®. It's a program you will be using many times for characterization, plotting, and dialogue help, and a number of other subjects that are designed to ease the path to publication. Both WritePro and FictionMaster have been selected by the Book-of-the-Month Club. Further information is available at 1-800-755-1124, or at http://www.writepro.com.

Help with Dialogue

Much help is available for this important subject. See Chapter Seven of this book. For additional guidance on dialogue, see Chapter Eleven of *Stein on Writing*, "The Secrets of Good Dialogue," and Chapter Seven, which describes the Actors Studio method for developing instant tension and drama; it makes writing adversarial dialogue much easier. If you want to revise and enhance your dialogue under my guidance, I refer you to the software program called FictionMaster; one of its four modules is entirely on dialogue and is of help to screenwriters and playwrights as well as novelists and short story writers. Information about FictionMaster is available at http://www.writepro.com.

"Dialogue for Writers" is an audiotape that contains the essence of the twelve-week, award-winning course I gave at the University of California. You can get the tape free if you order FictionMaster or WritePro by calling 1-800-755-1124 during eastern business hours and mention that I said not to charge you for the tape. Thousands of writers have this tape, and some play the tape over and over again in their cars. If you're a beginner, you'll find elementary instruction on dialogue in the WritePro program, described on the website http://www.writepro.com. While you're there, check out the section that contains advice I gave some famous writers.

Help on Flashbacks

Chapter Fourteen of *Stein on Writing* shows you how to bring background material into the foreground, avoiding flashbacks. If you must use a flashback, that chapter shows how to segue into and out of the flashback for the least possible interruption of the reader's experience.

Help from Independent Editors

They used to be called "book doctors," a term probably derived from "play doctors." Experienced playwrights, some as famous as Thornton Wilder, would view a play in rehearsal that needed fixing and make suggestions.

Some decades back if your work was talented and thought to be eventually publishable, your book could be bought and an editor assigned to work with you on its revision. As bottom-line management took over most publishing houses, detailed and especially prolonged editing was viewed as not cost-effective for most novels, and agents were expected to submit manuscripts that were as final as possible. That change occasioned the development of a new profession, independent editors, mainly individuals who are experienced editors or writers or both, who evaluate and work on manuscripts, helping the authors bring them up to speed. That help does not come cheap, but the hourly rates are a lot lower than, say, lawyers charge. Many book doctors charge by the assignment, whether it's an evaluation, a long memo of recommendations, or actual line-editing of an entire manuscript. Some book doctors advertise in *Writer's Digest*, some do not advertise anywhere. I can only refer writers to the small number of book doctors whose work I know. Online, go to http://www.writepro.com, and from the menu on the left, click on "Book Doctors." You can also obtain a list of independent editors, with addresses and phone numbers, by phoning (914) 762-1255 during eastern business hours and asking that the Book Doctor List be sent to you. It's free.

Help for the Computerless

If you don't use a computer and you want help on any aspect of writing, you can still get the benefit of the 1998 Fiction Weekend on six audiotapes that were recorded during this two-day session, attended by forty-eight professionals and newcomers from all parts of the United States and Canada. The program covered can also be seen on http://www.writepro.com on the Internet. If you don't have access to the Internet, descriptive material is available by calling 1-800-755-1124.

Help with Legal Issues

I'm not a lawyer, but I sometimes get inquiries about legal issues. The book I refer writers to has the unwieldy title *The Copyright Permission and Libel Handbook*, with the subtitle *A Step-by-Step Guide for Writers, Editors, and Publishers.* The authors, both lawyers, are Lloyd J. Jassin and Steven C. Schechter. The publisher is John Wiley & Sons. The title makes it sound like a book for specialists, though it is in fact a treasure for writers and quite easy to understand. For instance, the book has a substantial section on "fair use," which means what and how much you can quote from someone else's work and avoid getting sued. This inexpensive paperback is worth keeping on a shelf within easy reach. One of the authors, Lloyd Jassin, knows publishing from the inside, which enhances the practicality of the information. Check out how to get information from the copyright office by modem and fax (it takes forever to get an answer by mail). The table of contents of this book runs to ten pages. Here are some of the subject categories I found useful:

Clearing Rights: An Overview
Copyright Basics
A Four-Factor Test for Determining Fair Use [quoting someone else's material]
Real-Life Examples of Fair Use and Foul Use
What Copyright Doesn't Protect
How to Get Permission to Use Material, Including Photographs, Charts, Figures, Music, Speeches, and Lots Else

How to Deal with Collaborators and Contributors
What Is a Work-for-hire, and How Can It Keep You from Ever Getting Royalties?
Multimedia Clearances
The Basics of Libel Law
Who Can Sue You and What Could They Get?
What If Someone Threatens to Sue You?

The appendixes are of value. They include sample forms for permissions and much else. The fourth appendix contains sample disclaimers and a knowledgeable disclaimer about disclaimers, a subject most writers don't understand. The fifth appendix usefully lists industry directories, trade and professional organizations (with addresses and phone numbers), copyright licensing organizations, voluntary legal assistance, and copyright and trademark search firms who can do the work for you.

Help with Nonfiction

All the chapters in Part IV of *Stein on Writing* are on nonfiction, including the use of fiction techniques to enhance nonfiction, using conflict, suspense, and tension in nonfiction, and how to deal with quoting people so it doesn't get boring. There are also seven other chapters that relate to nonfiction as well as fiction.

Many journalists, biographers, and nonfiction article writers have used my computer program FirstAid for Writers®, which contains an entire module on nonfiction, and has been around for nearly a decade. Unfortunately, it's still a DOS and Mac program, but an advanced version in Windows has been promised. A road map showing all of the sections of FirstAid for Writers is available free from WritePro's headquarters, at 914-755-1124. Gossip: One of the big resellers of software told us that a lot of people who order the program do so because it contains two sections on erotic writing.

Help with Particularity

Most writers starting out are told to be concrete rather than general. I have always been uncomfortable with that because it isn't specific enough. I developed the idea of particularity, which seems to have been much more helpful to writers. Chapter Twenty-nine of *Stein on Writing* is on that subject. There is also a section on particularity in FictionMaster's fourth module ("Overcoming Obstacles to Publication") that enables me to guide writers on their own work. For more information via the Internet, click on FictionMaster at http://www/writepro.com.

Help with Plotting

For additional plotting advice, refer to Chapters Six, Seven, and Eight of *Stein on Writing.* Note especially the kind of plots that interest readers the most, described in Chapter Six, "Thwarting Desire: The Basics of Plotting." Chapter Seven, "The Actors Studio Method for Developing Drama in Plots," describes a method that enables you to create tension between characters quickly. It's been extraordinarily useful to a number of writers I've worked with. Chapter Eight deals with "The Crucible," a principle that has been useful to some classic and some recent writers you have likely read, and not coincidentally helped me write a novel that sold over a million copies. The crucible idea is useful, and I urge you to familiarize yourself with it.

If you need my help in planning or revising a plot, one of FictionMaster's four modules is entirely on plotting, and is of value to screenwriters and playwrights as well as novelists. Information about FictionMaster is available on the Internet at http://www.writepro.com, and also by phone at 1-800-755-1124.

Help with Point of View

Even longtime professionals have problems with point of view. Chapter Thirteen of *Stein on Writing* deals with the basics at length. Chapter Eight of this book deals with more-complex variants. Some writers find that the quasi-interactive teaching method employed in Module 4 of FictionMaster helps clarify point-of-view issues in relation to their own work. Tight control of point of view is not easy. Writers have told me that two of my novels have been helpful in understanding the more complex forms of point of view, *Other People* and *The Best Revenge.* Sadly, both are out of print at the moment, but used copies may be located on bibliofind.com. I'm told there is a plot afoot to get my out-of-print novels back into print early in the new millennium. We shall see.

Help with Information About the Publishing Process and Getting Published

To understand the whole process and how to deal with it, I recommend Judith Applebaum's valuable book, *How to Get Happily Published.* It has sold over half-a-million copies, which is one indicator of how many people are trying to write for publication. The book is available in both hardcover and paperback in many stores, and online. Try to get the latest edition. Check out www.happilypublished.com.

Michael Seidman has been an editor for thirty years. His advice to writers on the Internet is frequent and frank. His book *Fiction: The Art and Craft of Writing and Getting Published* (Pomegranate Press, 1999) has eight chapters on the publishing process, as well as much advice on the craft of fiction. You can sample excerpts at http://members.aol.com/michaelsei/book.htm. Pay special attention to what he says about category fiction if that's what you're writing.

Reference Books

Once upon a time I published Eric Partridge, the greatest lexicographer to create important works alone since Samuel Johnson. Pride in making a success of his etymological dictionary, *Origins*, did not provide me with any special expertise in his subject. I use *The American Heritage Dictionary of the English Language* daily, my only weight-lifting exercise. It's published by Houghton Mifflin.

Frequent use of a thesaurus is a necessity for any writer. I've given up on the electronic ones, but use most often the paperback of *Roget's Super Thesaurus*, second edition, by Marc McCutcheon, of which I've bought several copies as gifts for writer friends. You don't have to look up a word in back in order to find what page in front to go to. It also contains antonyms of selected words. My backup thesaurus is J. I. Rodale's *The Synonym Finder*, which says it contains two-and-a-half times more words that the McCutcheon, but the type is smaller, and my eyes are older. I still find it useful sometimes to check one thesaurus against another.

A book not well enough known by writers is Penguin's *Dictionary of Literary Terms and Literary Theory* by J. A. Cuddon, now in its third edition. If you were educated anytime in the last half century, you'll find a lot you may not know under "Novel." It contains much erudition and gossip as well as explanations of literary and some not-so-literary terms. I prefer the definitions in my glossary, short and useful, but this Penguin volume is comprehensive and scholarly enough to fill over one thousand pages, and is surprisingly inexpensive in paperback.

Help with Revising and Perfecting Drafts

Much of what I've seen in print on this subject is wrongheaded. The efficient method I call Triage is described in detail in Chapter Thirty-two of *Stein on Writing*, and can save a writer months of life. That book also contains a chapter on revising nonfiction.

Help with Subject Matter for Fiction

Dramatic heat generated by cultural differences, inherited or nurtured, added to differences in individual temperaments, can help writers create wonderful stories. These differences are a valuable resource for scenes as well as entire plots, and are the underlying basis of conflict in fiction. For an understanding of this subject, you can start with Chapter Five of *Stein on Writing*, "Markers: The Key to Swift Characterization." FictionMaster contains two extensive sections on markers, one for characterization and one for plotting. National Book Award–winner Paul Fussell has an entertaining book called *Class: A Guide Through the American Status System* that is a stimulating source for the writer of fiction.

Help with Suspense

Chapter Nine of *Stein on Writing* covers the subject of keeping the reader reading throughout a whole book. Many beginning writers are not aware of the basic methods of creating suspense despite its use in most successful novels. Chapter Ten of *Stein on Writing*, "The Adrenaline Pump: Creating Tension," should be read in conjunction with your study of suspense technique because tension and suspense are not the same and are created differently.

Help with Titles

This subject is more important than most writers think. Some books have succeeded because of their titles. Poor titles hurt good books. For starters, try Chapter Twenty-three of *Stein on Writing*, "The Door to Your Book: Titles That Attract." Material on titles also appears in the computer programs.

Help at Writers' Conferences

My writing students consistently tell me that they find writers' conferences beneficial in ways that I had not originally suspected.

Since writing is experienced by many as a lonely activity, writers-in-training enjoy the camaraderie of other writers as much as they do the instruction they receive in workshops. If you are relatively inexperienced in the commercial end of writing, writers conferences are also a good place to hear agents and editors talk. The fact that writers keep coming back to the same conferences year after year attests to their usefulness. *The Complete Guide to Writers Groups, Conferences, and Workshops* by Eileen Malone, published by Wylie, can be helpful. Malone has some interesting comments.

If you're planning to go to a conference at some distance, it's a good idea to check with one or two people who've been there. A way of getting a rounded picture is to ask a previous attendee what he or she liked best about the conference, and then ask them what was worst. If they deny there's anything bad, ask what's least good. Candor has to be pried out of some people.

GLOSSARY OF TERMS USED BY WRITERS AND EDITORS
(revised 1999)

Architecture: In fiction, the design of a larger work such as a novel, the purposeful order of scenes.

Aria: In any writing, a longer speech designed to evoke an increasing emotional effect on the reader or viewer. See "Speechifying."

Backstory: The characters' lives before the story, novel, or film began.

Chapter: Part of a longer work that is set off with a number or a title. It may have several scenes or scenelets.

Cliche: A hackneyed expression, tired from overuse.

Coincidence: In fiction, something that happens by chance and is insufficiently motivated.

Crucible: In fiction, a situation or locale that holds characters together as their conflict heats up. Their motivation to continue opposing each other is greater than their motivation or ability to escape.

Description: A depiction of a locale or person within a story. The Latin root of the word "depiction," *pingere*, means "to picture" or to fashion a visual image.

Diction: Choice of words, probably the best identifier of quality in writing.

Eccentricity: An offbeat manner of behavior, dress, or speech peculiar to a person and dissimilar to the same characteristics of most other people.

Echo: In dialogue, an answer that repeats all or part of the question.

Engine, Starting of: The moment when the reader's curiosity is so aroused that he will not put the book down or turn to something else. It usually carries an intimation of conflict, a character threatened or wanting something badly that he can't have.

Envelope: In fiction, a "container" provided by the author to be filled in by the reader's imagination. "Grandma sat staring out of the window" is visual, devoid of particulars, but from the context, the reader will imagine what she might be seeing.

Episodic: In fiction, a story told in parts in which one event happens after another without seeming to be integrated into the whole.

Explication: Undesirable information for the reader. Showing is good, telling is not as good, explication is worse.

Flab: Extraneous words, phrases, and other material that weaken the effect.

Flashback: A scene that precedes the time of the present story.

Handle: A short description of the book designed to evoke interest in it.

Immediate Scene: An action that happens in front of the reader, that is shown rather than told about. If you can't film a scene, it is not immediate. Theater, a truly durable art, consists almost entirely of immediate scenes.

Jargon: Words or expressions developed for use within a group that bar outsiders from readily understanding what is being said. The purpose of language is to communicate or evoke; jargon obfuscates or hides.

Line Space: Four blank lines in a double-spaced manuscript, used within chapters to indicate a break, usually of time, or a shift to a different location.

Marker: An easily identified signal that reveals a character's social or cultural class, heredity, or upbringing.

Metaphor: A figure of speech that results when words or phrases are brought together that do not ordinarily belong together, yet by their proximity convey a fresh meaning. Some of the best novel titles are metaphors (e.g., *The Heart Is a Lonely Hunter*).

Motivation: The source that impels an action, the reason that something is done.

Narrative Summary: The recounting of what happens offstage, out of the reader's sight and hearing, an event that is told about rather than shown.

Oblique: In dialogue, an indirect reply not in line with the preceding speech, not directly responsive.

Omen: A portent of something to come, usally something bad. An "omen" should not be confused with "telegraphing," which is less subtle and tells the reader of a future event before it happens.

Omniscient: The point of view in which the author roams everywhere, including the minds of all the characters.

One plus one equals one-half: (Also 1+1=1/2) A formula designed to remind writers that conveying the same matter more than once in different words diminishes the effect of what is said. A corollary of this equation is that if the same matter is said in two different ways, either alone has a stronger effect.

Particularity: A precisely observed detail rather than a generality.

Planting: In fiction, plays, and film, "planting" means preparing the ground for something that comes later, usually to make the later action credible.

Point of View: The perspective from which a scene is written; which character's eyes and mind are witnessing the events.

Scene: A unit of writing, usually an integral incident with a beginning and end that in itself is not isolable as a story. It is visible to the reader or audience as an event that can be witnessed, almost always involving two or more characters, dialogue, and action in a single setting.

Segue: Derived from music, it means to glide as unobtrusively as possible into something new.

Showing: Making action visible to the reader as if it were happening before his eyes, moment by moment.

Simile: A figure of speech in which two unlike things are compared, linked by *as* or *like*. A simile shows the similarity of two things not previously connected.

Speech Signature: Within dialogue, a tag that is characteristic of the speaker, such as Jay Gatsby's "old sport."

Speechifying: Monologue that runs too long.

Static: Describes a scene lacking visible action or dialogue that moves a story forward.

Suspense: The arousal and sustaining of curiosity as long as possible. It involves anticipation and sometimes anxiety about what is going to happen.

Tags: The means by which a speaker is identified, most commonly "he said" or "she said."

Telegraphing: Telling the reader of a future event before it happens, usually to be avoided. See "Omen."

Telling: Relating what happened offstage.

Tension: Moments of anxious uncertainty. Derived from the Latin *tendere*, meaning "to stretch."

Transition: A smooth link between between subjects, which avoids a sense of jumping from one topic to another.